Dreamworks

A Meeting of Spirituality and Psychology

Steve Price is a minister of the Uniting Church. He has a growing interest in Jungian psychology, therapy and counselling. He is especially concerned with the relationship between psychology, theology and spirituality.

David Haynes is a psychologist and Jungian therapist. He currently practises in Adelaide and is a lecturer in psychology at the University of South Australia

Dreamworks

A Meeting of Spirituality and Psychology

Steve Price and David Haynes

HarperCollins*Religious*
An imprint of HarperCollins*Publishers*

Published by HarperCollins*Religious*

HarperCollins*Publishers* (Australia) Pty Limited Group

17–19 Terracotta Drive

Blackburn, Victoria 3130

ACN 008 431 730

© Copyright Stephen Price and David Haynes, 1997

Copyright for illustrations reproduced remain with the individual artist.

All rights reserved. Except as provided by Australian copyright law, no part of this book may be reproduced or transmitted by any form or by any means, electronic or mechanical, including photocopying, recording, or by any information storage or retrieval system, without permission in writing from the publishers.

First published 1997

Text designed by Tony Gilevski

Cover designed by Tony Gilevski

Cover illustration by Robbie Marantz/The Image Bank – all rights reserved.

Typeset in Apollo by J&M Typesetting

Printed in Australia by Australian Print Group

The National Library in Australia

Cataloguing-in-Publication data:

Price, Steve, 1957– .

   Dreamworks: a meeting of spirituality and psychology.

   Bibliography.

   ISBN 1 86371 680 7.

   1. Dreams – Religious aspects. 2. Dreams – Psychological aspects. I. Haynes, David, 1939– . II. Title.

154.63

Our thanks go to those who have given us permission to reproduce copyright material in this book. All rights of copyright holders are reserved. Particular sources of print material are acknowledged in the text. Every effort has been made to trace the original source material contained in this book. Where the attempt has been unsuccessful, the publishers would be pleased to hear from the author/publisher to rectify any omission.

The author and publishers wish to thank and acknowledge the following for use of copyright material: Jung, CG, *Collected Works*. Copyright © 1983 by PUP. Reprinted by permissions Princeton University Press. Jung CG, *Modern Man in Search of a Soul*, Copyright © 1933 by Routledge, London. Ormstein, Robert, *The Psychology of Consciousness*, Penguin Books London. Howe L, 'Dream Interpretation in Spiritual Guidance,' *Journal of Spiritual Care*. Michael Leunig for the 'The Dream' poem and illustration, 'Dear God' poem and illustration.

The Scripture quotations contained herein are from the New Revised Standard Version of the Bible, copyrighted, 1989, by the Division of Christian Education of the National Council of Churches in the United States of America, and are used by permission. All rights reserved.

CONTENTS

Foreword	ix
Acknowledgments	xv
1 'Dream Believing'	1
Spirituality and Dreams	2
Alternate Realities?	4
The Dreams of Antiquity	4
Dreams in a Technological Culture	6
Dreams and Spirituality	8
2 Dream Theory	13
The Physiology of Dreaming	13
Dream Reality	15
3 Dreams and the Hebrew Scriptures	21
The Dream: Revelation for Community	21
Early Hebrew Tradition	23
The Role of the Prophet	23
Dreams that Shape History	24
Dream or Vision?	28
4 Dreams and the Christian Era	31
Dreams and the New Testament	31
The Early Christian Communities	34
The Evolution of Christian Thought about Dreams	35

	The Loss of a Dreamwork Tradition	37
	The Rise of Rationalism and the Decline of the Dream	38
5	**The Early Psychologists**	41
	The Legacy of Freud, Jung and the Early Psychologists	42
6	**A Modern Dreaming**	53
	Are Some Dreams of Divine Origin?	53
	Divine, Numinous or Encounter Dreams	54
	Prophetic Dreams	55
	The Difficulties of Discernment	56
	The Inner, or Personal Dream	57
	Integrating the Personal and the Divine	58
	Psychology and Spirituality	58
	Spirituality, Community and Justice	59
7	**The Language of Dreams**	65
	Jung's Theory of Archetypes	70
8	**The Shadow**	75
9	**Animus and Anima**	81
10	**The Great Mother; The Great Father**	89
	The Great Father Archetype	89
	The Great Mother Archetype	90
11	**Other Archetypes**	101
	The Child	101
	The Hero/Heroine	103
	The Trickster	105
	Death or the Night Journey: The Inner Journey	106
	The Wise, Old Person	107
	The Persona	108
12	**The Self**	111
	The Jungian Concept of Healthy Development	111
	Transitions of Spiritual/Faith Development	115
	The Self and the God-image	116
13	**Steps of the Life Journey through Dreams**	121
	Two Beginning Dreams	121
	Shadow and Anima/Animus Dreams	124
	The Abandoned Child and the Wise Woman	127
	The Night Journey and Transformation	129

14 Dream Interpretation	**135**
Working with your Dreams	135
Rules to Help in the Interpretation of Dreams	139
Using Active Imagination in Dreamwork	145
Drawing	148
The Use of Ritual	148
Group Work	151
Additional Guidelines for Spiritual Development and Dreamwork	153
Your Dream Therapist or Guide	155
15 Remembering Dreams	**161**
Resources for Further Reflection	**166**
A. Glossary of Common Psychological Terms	166
B. Recommended Further Reading List	168
C. Sample Rituals	170
D. Biblical References: Dreams	172
E. Biblical References: Visions	179
Index	**187**

FOREWORD

In George Bernard Shaw's play *St Joan*, Joan claims that the voices she hears telling her what to do come from God. Her interrogator Captain Robert de Baudricourt, correcting her, states 'They come from your imagination'. Joan boldly replies 'Of course. That is how the messages of God come to us.' At this point, another character, Bertrand de Poulengey interjects: 'Checkmate'.

There is an intuitive truthfulness in this statement put in the mouth of Joan that asserts that the messages of God can come through the human imagination. C.G. Jung writes that 'it would be blasphemy to assert that God can manifest himself everywhere save only in the human soul. Indeed the very intimacy of the relationship between God and the soul precludes from the start any devaluation of the latter'[1]. So Jung goes on to argue that the soul must contain in itself the faculty of relationship to God, which, in psychological terms, corresponds to the archetype of the God-image, which he also calls the Self. The Self is the real foundation of the human personality.

Given the negative attitude towards the imagination and the suspicion towards and devaluation of the world of dreams which our era has inherited, it may be surprising to learn that people of undoubted spirituality in the religious traditions of both the East and West, have often been influenced and indeed guided by the visual imagery which they experienced in sleep (dreams) or in the waking state (visions).

In many biblical stories, which Steve Price and David Haynes draw our attention to in this book, and in the lives of holy people, one reads often of dreams and visions which were taken as guidance from God. I have always been impressed that it was a vision which Peter experienced while at prayer just before lunch at Jaffa, which led to the broadening of consciousness of the early Christians to enable them to welcome pagans into the community which until then had consisted of Jewish Christians only. In the trice repeated vision, reported in Acts of the Apostles chapter 10, a big sheet was lowered to earth containing every kind of animal, and a voice said 'Peter, kill and eat'. Peter as an observer of the Jewish law, refuses, and is told 'What God has made clean, you have no right to call profane'. Soon after this experience Peter baptised the first Gentile into the Christian community — Cornelius the Roman centurian.

The authors of *DreamWorks* show the ancient tradition of the importance of dreams and visions and their interpretation in the early Hebrew Scriptures. They trace the development and vicissitudes of this ancient heritage through the Hebrew Scriptures, through the inter-testamental period, through the time of the New Testament and the early Christian community, and briefly touch on later aspects of Western intellectual development which relate to their theme. They highlight the pivotal times where this ancient heritage got lost along the way and was replaced by a prejudice against imagination, to which we in the 20th century have been heir. In presenting the material of our western Judeo-Christian tradition, they show us the life that pulsates within it, and the nourishment it can give to the soul of people of the 20th century whether alienated from their soul-tradition or not.

They introduce the work of the pioneers of modern depth psychology: Sigmund Freud, Alfred Adler and C.G. Jung, who did so much to restore the importance of the human imagination and specifically the dream to the consciousness of 20th century people — beginning in 1900 with the publication of *The Interpretation of Dreams* by Freud. There follows a more detailed presentation of the Psychology of C.G. Jung over several chapters.

The authors obviously draw on their practical experience of working with people in ministry and psychotherapy, interweaving spiritual with psychological insights in their text. They present their material in non-technical terms where possible, using their own words to describe and understand the rich data of inner experience. They give many excellent examples of dreams and the understandings they have reached about the meanings of those dreams with the dreamers. They wrestle with questions and common misconceptions and misunderstandings about dreams and dreamwork, giving practical guidelines and pointers for best understanding the phenomena of the unconscious and helpful suggestions for dealing with them.

They warn about the common pitfalls encountered in inner work: especially the danger of neglecting the opportunity for inner development and growth in self-knowledge by short-circuiting the psychological process and acting out emotional impulses without insight or reflection in the outer world. These impulses and energies rather need our inner attention and loving acceptance, so that they can be transformed, and by integration lead us to greater wholeness of personality. They also constantly remind the reader to take the dream symbolically and not literally — for the language of the soul is symbolical: the images of our dreams point beyond themselves to intangible but very real factors of our inner life which are still not conscious to us — unconscious feelings, emotions, thoughts and attitudes. The dream should lead us within where they shed light on what goes on behind the scenes of our lives. Then armed with the knowledge of our inner life, we can live our lives more consciously and responsibly, and come closer to fulfilling the innate pattern of our individual being in the conduct of our lives.

The final chapter of *DreamWorks* contains a glossary which deals with technical terms of psychology which are used in the book; a comprehensive recommended reading list for those who wish to pursue some aspect of the work further; two delightful and satisfying rituals around dream work; and finally a very valuable list of references to dreams and visions in the Bible, which summarises in a nutshell the riches of our Judeo-Christian sacred tradition in regard to the theme of dreams and visions.

I can only agree wholeheartedly and fully endorse the underlying conviction of the authors that there is no substantial conflict between psychological growth and spiritual development. As human beings and Christians — or people following any of the great spiritual traditions — our task today is to make conscious and embrace all aspects of ourselves (even the most undesirable) with a Christian charity which extends even to the most dangerous enemy, the one within: for left to itself, out of touch with human consciousness, this enemy within is the source of all the woes that beset humankind. This demands an attitude which is neither puritanical nor self-indulgent, but deeply aware of and accepting of all that is within us, all the contrary aspects of our nature. Jung advocates patience and 'being Christian on the inside' (ie. in loving the enemy). One needs to accept the pattern of one's personality and fulfil it — even accepting one's sinfulness. This deep self-acceptance mellows the personality, and 'the gold begins to glow… (for) people who can agree with themselves are like gold'[2]. Because one has made peace with oneself, one doesn't need to act out destructively in the outer world and so one lives much more ethically than the person who is at odds with him or herself.

In his poem *The Dark Night*, the 16th century Spanish spiritual director and mystic John of the Cross speaks of the inner light that guided him to the inner meeting with, and experience of Christ, the Beloved of the soul:

> *On that glad night... ...*
> *With no other light or guide*
> *Than the one that burned in my heart;*
>
> *This guided me*
> *More surely that the light of noon*
> *To where he was awaiting me....*[3]

Here he gives utterance to his own experience of the inner journey at a time of greatest darkness when he was guided only by the inner light. For people alive to the inner world, this light that burns in the heart is a surer and more individual guide as they make their way through life than the 'light of noon' — the sun which shines on all, the collective conventional wisdom, the way society thinks people should act. It is our life's task to protect, foster and nurture this holy inward consciousness with all the means at our disposal — for example, prayer, meditation, reflection, recollection, dream work, ethical living etc. — all the things which represent the oil which is needed to keep the lamp burning (cf. the parable of the wise and foolish virgins in Matthew 25). We must learn to trust this inner light of the heart and be guided by it in the conduct of our lives. I would suggest that the light of our true nature shines through our dreams, balancing our distorted attitudes, calling us back to ourselves when we have lost touch with our truest feelings, giving us images for our states of mind thus enabling their transformation, and shedding light on urgent issues of our personality and the most impossible conflicts of practical life.

Jung sees the dream as a little hidden door in the innermost and most secret recesses of the soul[4] and a most immediate approach to the world of inner experience. Working with one's dreams is a way of listening deeply to oneself, of investigating one's nature, and of getting one's bearings, for its imagery reveals our psychological situation with absolute candour and veracity in a most factual way.

I see no real conflict ultimately between spiritual development and Jungian psychological development for the person committed to inner growth: nor between spiritual direction given in the context of a faith community and psychological therapy and guidance at this level of work with the energies of the unconscious. At a certain level, it seems more a matter of perspective and emphasis — even one of language — for it seems we are talking about the same inner reality and process, which makes all the difference to outer life.

In religious language, the spiritual director is reminded, for example, by John of the Cross that he or she 'is not the chief agent, guide and mover of souls, but that the principal guide is the Holy Spirit'. The director's task should not be to accommodate people to his or her own method and condition, but rather to 'observe the road along which God is leading them, and if he does not recognise it, he should leave them alone and not bother them'[5]. John of the Cross continues that the director's task at a certain stage of spiritual development is to disencumber the soul and bring it into solitude and idleness and free it of all things, so that it is empty (for God does not fit into an occupied heart), so that God can communicate Himself to it silently and secretly.

At this stage of the spiritual life the person can only prepare himself or herself for the work of God in the depths of their being — for the most delicate, sublime and hidden anointings and shadings of the Holy Spirit, as John of the Cross so beautifully puts it[6]. Living the will of God in every moment of their lives becomes the main concern of the person and their source of joy and peace.

In Jungian psychological language, the analyst or therapist is urged to work with the client's dreams and other phenomena of the unconscious (visions, fantasies, emotional reactions) in order to get a sense of the purposefulness in the psychic life of the person, for healing comes from within. The dreams seem best understood as a manifestation of the meaningful inner balancing of the psychic life of the person; they seem to have their source in the dynamic self-regulating centre of the personality, which is called the Self or the archetype of the God-image. They manifest a secret purpose which is deeper and more adamant than the purposes of the ego. If this secret purpose is met on the inside, it can lead to growth; if one refuses, one often meets this deeper purpose on the outside as a difficult fate in life (e.g. a major illness, a serious accident). Conscientious work on the dreams reveals this deeper purpose of the Self in the person and the analyst's task is to help the person to recognise it and co-operate with it in everyday life. So, for example, the person who dreams of the death of some figure who represents old rigid habitual attitudes of mind, needs to examine where those old attitudes are operative in life, and investigate where they can be let go, leaving space for new freer attitudes and deeper identity to emerge. As the person works with their unconscious, taking its demands more and more into account in everyday life, the centre of gravity of the total personality shifts its position — from the ego, the centre of consciousness, to the Self, the centre of the total personality, and the person lives in a more truly centred way[7].

Both perspectives point to the reality of a deeper process in the human being which director and therapist try to make space for and to which they direct the attention of the person, so that the inner process does not get crowded out of the consciousness of the person by the demands of outer life. It is a question of listening to the deepest and most whole and sound part of the person. In this way the gradual transformation of the life-difficulties of the person can take place according to the laws of the human psyche, and is revealed for instance in images of death and rebirth. This mystery of the transformation of human consciousness finds confirmation in the saying of Christ, referring to his imminent death and resurection, in John 12:24: 'Unless a grain of wheat falls into the earth and dies, it remains alone; but if it dies, it bears much fruit'.

I heartily commend this book to those people who feel called to embark on the great adventure of the inner journey of self discovery, especially those who are concerned to integrate the findings of modern depth psychology with their faith tradition.

Terence McBride
Arncliffe NSW
November 1996

References

[1] Jung, C.G., 1974, *Psychology and Alchemy, Collected Works volume 12*, Princeton N.J.: Princeton University Press, p.10.
[2] Jung, C.G., 1989, *Nietzsche's Zarathustra, The Seminars, volume two, part II*, London: Rouledge, p. 803.
[3] St John of the Cross, 1991, *The Dark Night, The Collected Works of St John of the Cross*, translated by Kavanaugh and Rodriguez, Revised Edition, Washington D.C.: Institute of Carmelite Studies, p.51.
[4] Cf. Jung, C.G., 1970, *Collected Works, 10: 144*, Princeton N.J: Princeton University Press.
[5] St John of the Cross, 1991, *Living Flame of Love, Collected Works*, translated by Kavanaugh and Rodriguez, Revised Edition, Washington D.C.: Institute of Carmelite Studies, p.691.
[6] Cf. St John of the Cross, op cit, p. 689.
[7] Cf. Jung, C.G., 1970, *Collected Works, 13: 45*, Princeton N.J.: Princeton University Press.

ACKNOWLEDGMENTS

The authors would like to thank Hugh McGinlay from JBCE who first suggested the idea of writing something on dreams and spirituality, and all the helpful staff at HarperCollins for their support and faith in this project. We would also wish to thank Libby Mortimer for proofreading our drafts, Christine Chapman for inspirational discussions, Brian Williams for providing the worksheet that we used while composing chapter fifteen, the Alberton/Port Adelaide Uniting Church Parish for providing freedom and encouragement during the writing period (and for their willingness in acting as guinea pigs from time to time!) and the many others who have helped, inspired and contributed to the adventure! And, finally, our wives and children, for their encouragement, support and patience throughout.

Dear God
We give thanks for the darkness of the night where lies the world of dreams. Guide us closer to our dreams so that we may be nourished by them. Give us good dreams and memory of them so that we may carry their poetry and mystery into our daily lives.
Grant us deep and restful sleep that we may wake refreshed with strength enough to renew a world grown tired. We give thanks for the inspiration of stars, the dignity of the moon and the lullabies of crickets and frogs.
Let us restore the night and reclaim it as a sanctuary of peace, where silence shall be music to our hearts and darkness shall throw light upon our souls. Good night.
Sweet dreams.
Amen.
Michael Leunig

1
'DREAM BELIEVING'

Among all my patients in the second half of life — that is to say, over thirty-five — there has not been one whose problem in the last resort was not that of finding a religious outlook on life. It is safe to say that every one of them fell ill because he had lost that which the living religions of every age have given to their followers, and none of them has been really healed who did not regain his religious outlook ... It is indeed high time for the clergy and the psychotherapist to join forces to meet this great spiritual task.

Carl Jung[1]

The family cat lies basking in the warm afternoon sun on the verandah. Its tail begins to move briskly from side to side, its paws and whiskers begin to twitch, and we tell our children that the cat is dreaming of chasing mice through the paddock.

A child wakes in the middle of the night, crying uncontrollably, sweaty and hot, full of fear and confusion. As they are comforted, a story unfolds of horrible monsters, chases through a forest, eyes glowing in the dark.

The elderly woman, lying in a hospital bed, slowly dying of cancer, dreams of her own mother, long since dead, cradling her in her arms and telling her the best is yet to come. She awakes, and to the amazement of the staff, has been transformed from a scared and bitter woman to one who is calm and relaxed, her eyes reflecting an inner serenity.

Dreams are all around us, yet what exactly are they? Are they merely our brains running in overdrive at the end of a busy day, or do our dreams provide a valuable resource for thinking about ourselves and life? Does God speak to people in dreams, or are they merely a biological hangover from our primitive origins? Should we be paying attention to our dreams, and, if so, how do we learn to understand them? Can we learn to dream more? Are there different sorts of dreams, and is it possible to tell the difference? Does a dream have one specific meaning, or a whole range of possibilities?

These are just some of the sorts of questions we will attempt to explore in this journey into the marvellous, confusing and complex pathways of the human mind.

Spirituality and Dreams

The growing interest in a variety of spiritual experience, and in psychology, reflects our deep need to make sense of our life experience, and to create meaning. One of the resources that we carry within us in the Western post-modern world is that of the Judaeo-Christian tradition. Many people have become sceptical of its relevance and content, yet perhaps a more careful examination of such traditions may disclose insights that will aid us on our present journey.

For many years, our traditions have been noticeable for their silence on the subject of dreams. Graham Wakefield's *Dictionary of Christian Spirituality*[2], now in its fifth edition, still does not have any reference to dreams.

Yet things are changing. In the last few years there has been a growing interest in the role of dreams, not just in the Christian tradition, but clearly in mainstream culture. Take a wander through your local bookstore, and you will discover a growing number of titles on dreams, dream interpretation, and the psychology and spirituality of dreaming.

A quick glance through the Bible will reveal that dreams were taken seriously by the writers and actors of Scripture. However, in many mainstream churches today, very little is said about dreams as part of Christian experience and spirituality. To turn up at work and talk about a dream you had the previous night may be met with amusement, ridicule, or, perhaps if you are particularly fortunate, interest and curiosity. The same is probably likely to happen at church!

In general, Christians seem to have adopted the rationalistic and materialistic view of the world that has been the dominant cultural perspective of the past few generations. Dreams are at best an amusing throwback to a primitive age, and at worst, the realm of the demonic. In order to avoid the dangers of an other-worldly Christianity with little or no relevance to everyday life, we have also rejected our inner worlds — the lands of dreams and imagination.

In addition, paying attention to dreams seems to be too close to a form of spiritism, and in Protestant traditions has often been expressed in terms of people opening themselves up to 'forces beyond their control'. When we look at some of the amazing characters and scenarios that occur in our dreams, it is easy to understand in part this fear, especially if we perceive dreams as being literal, not symbolic.

The erotic content, too, of many dreams, has made those of a religious orientation uncomfortable. If we have an erotic dream, have we committed a sin? Many Christians, for example, find their dreams deeply disturbing at times, and without helpful tools to understand their dreams, and with very little acknowledgment of the positive importance of dreams, do not know what to do. They are therefore resigned to suffer silently a debilitating sense of guilt, or simply dismiss their dreams as the result of too many chilli and ginger prawns the night before!

This has left the world of dreams the domain of groups who use dreams as communications from God in a very literal sense, along with all the dangers that such literalism may involve. A dream of killing someone is not necessarily a command from God to enact the event in the physical world, yet this is the implication of literal interpretation. Taking events and characters literally may be foolish and even dangerous.

However, if we come to appreciate dreams as primarily symbolic language, far richer resources for our lives, and our spiritual growth, can be liberated. We will need to rediscover the tools that can help us take our dreams seriously, yet prevent us from being overtaken by the psychic energy that can be unleashed.

This is not to say that we might never have a clear message from God, but rather that the common language of dreams is symbolic, and there will be the challenge to try and discern potentially different types of dreams. This differentiation is possibly why ancient traditions often had several different words to describe dream-like material (e.g. a vision or oracle was not an ordinary dream, even when encountered during sleep).

Literalism also contains within it the premise that dreams have only one specific meaning. This is rarely the case, for they may contain a variety of meanings, requiring layers of interpretation. The most immediately obvious meaning may well hide a far more significant, but overlooked, meaning. The time, place, context and events of our lives will also affect understanding a dream.

Therefore, two basic principles of commonsense dreamwork are that the imagery is (a) symbolic and (b) may contain layers of meaning.

Alternate Realities?

The symbolic nature of dreams is also a recognition that there is more to life than what we tend to experience as the 'concrete' world. In our culture today, the 'real world' has come to mean the physical world, and it is only in this world that we believe we can gain knowledge, learn about human behaviour, and form relationships. Yet as we will discover, this attitude to life is a relatively recent Western phenomenon, and many people are beginning to question such an outlook.

At the heart of the issue are the questions 'What is a human being?' and 'What is reality?'. Primitive or pre-literate societies took dreams extremely seriously, even to the point where there was very little separation of the world of dreams and the physical world. What was perceived in dreams and through imagination was taken as being a valid reality, as much as the physical world was real. A figure appearing in a dream was 'real', and the challenge or insight brought by the figure needed to be dealt with. Many societies had well-developed systems for interpreting and recording dreams, as well as techniques for encouraging them (including the use of narcotics) and for dispelling them. Some societies had people set aside to help interpret dreams; in others it was a community activity. In some North American Indian communities, it was not possible to become an adult until a person experienced a dream that revealed something about their identity and future role in the tribe.

Time was seen as cyclical, rather than linear, and underpinned this integration of differing realities. Dreaming, then, was seen as a normal and significant human activity that provided a resource for understanding the individual and the community.

The Dreams of Antiquity

If dreams then were an alternate, yet valid reality, they were also seen as an arena where the Divine was at work. Dreams were seen to have their origins in the gods, in North American native cultures, and also in Egyptian, Greek and Roman cultures, and this is generally true for most others. As we will see in the following chapters, in the Bible dreams were seen to be spiritual in nature, and messages from God.

The Egyptian 'Beatty' Papyrus, thought to be written around 1350 BCE, records over two hundred dreams, mostly from royalty. The dreams are generally interpreted as communications or commands from the gods, and the papyrus also includes instructions for dispelling unpleasant dreams.

In Asia, dreams were seen as the product of the soul leaving the body and wandering in a spirit world. Such wandering might reveal something of the future, and suggest an appropriate course of action.

Across different cultures, similar dream symbols might be interpreted in different ways, reflecting the varying status and mythology that was attached to a particular symbol. For example, to encounter a snake in a dream was a potential omen of impending sickness for a Greek, but the same symbol was believed to have a positive value for Assyrian, Jewish and Egyptian people.

The ancient Greeks would take their dreams to seers and oracles for interpretation, and there was the expectation that those of wisdom would have dreams. People actively sought dreams, and would fast, abstain from sex and alcohol, in the hope of creating an altered state of consciousness more conducive to dreams. (At other times, the same activities were used to prevent dreams!)

When suffering from an unknown disease, a person might spend the night in a temple of the god Asclepius, in the hope of a dream, which, when interpreted, would reveal the nature and treatment of the condition.

A distinction was also made between different types of dreams — some being oracles, omens and messages, others the product of the day's affairs, or 'ordinary' dreams. Omens were clearly messages from the gods, and needed to be acted upon. Ordinary dreams could be good or bad, the good being sent from the gods, the bad from demons. There was a thriving business in sorting out one from the other, and then responding with an appropriate ritual.

The Romans continued the tradition of taking dreams seriously; so seriously in fact that Augustus passed a law compelling anyone who dreamed about the nation to retell it publicly. Several emperors, including Tiberius, Caligula and Domitian, had their deaths foretold in dreams.

In both the Greek and Roman traditions, however, there began to appear more discussion about what exactly dreams were, and there emerged differing viewpoints, ranging from those that upheld the 'traditional' divine value, to ones searching for physical causes, to those such as the one held by Xenophenes, who dismissed dreams out of hand.

Socrates thought that dreams were the voice of the conscience, and Plato, forshadowing some of the concepts of Freud, believed they were repressed urges taking form during sleep. Other classical writers held to the view that they were messages from the gods. Aristotle may have also felt them to be caused by the body's movement in sleep, and Lucretius thought they were actual objects shed from the particles of other material objects into the air.

Cicero was sceptical about the value of dreams, especially as a medium of divine revelation. If the gods wished to communicate with people, surely it would make more sense to do it during wakefulness than through the uncertainty of a dream? And, he argued, dreams must all come from God, or none do. If the latter, then they are not worthy of any attention.

All of these varying concepts and ideas, and the different values given to dreams, were part of the environment that would go on to influence the status of dreams in emerging Christianity, and become part of its legacy in the modern world.

Dreams in a Technological Culture

The range of opinions above about the significance of dreams appears to be a forerunner of the sorts of views people have today. If some dreams are 'rubbish', then surely all are? If God wishes to speak to us, why in a dream, open to misinterpretation? Or perhaps there is a middle ground, where dreams may reveal something about the dreamer, on exceptional occasions be prophetic or divine, and sometimes be nothing at all?

Even with such strong traditions of including dreams as part of the material with which we can work psychologically and spiritually, somewhere along the line we have lost ready access to this resource.

Perhaps our simplistic, 'folk' interpretation of the scientific method, and the rise of rationalism, is to blame. The more sophisticated and technologically developed our society becomes, the more we wish to deny anything that suggests that there may be more to life than meets the eye. Being sophisticated is seen to exclude spirituality and mysticism.

But the rise of rationalism and reductionism does not seem to have dispelled the human need for a spiritual dimension to life, and a sense of connection with 'otherness'. Despite a scientific and technological environment, superstition, as well as spirituality, is alive and well. We will pray the car will start on a cold morning, thank God for the green light on the way to work, step warily around the ladder on the footpath, think twice about entering the lift with a black cat sitting in it, and, having finally arrived in the office, pull out the paper and check our horoscope for the day. Then we'll ring a friend and make arrangements for a Bible study group the next night!

Therefore, it appears as if we hold two opposing philosophies. Our day-to-day lives are very much the product of a scientific and technological society, but when we scratch away at the surface, we discover a deep residue of diverse beliefs, superstitions and values that would seem to be at odds with a totally rational world. This seems to point to a basic human need to connect with something beyond ourselves, which aids us in making sense of what we experience, but also helps us interpret our feelings and emotions.

It is probably this strange, yet not surprising, mix of spirituality and superstition, present in a post-industrial world, that makes dreamwork difficult not just for Christians and others seeking a spiritual framework, but for most people. Much of our energy has been spent trying to come to terms with this peculiar way of thinking, and, for people of faith, separating them, so that we might have faith that is centred and cohesive rather than based in magic or tradition. For some, taking dreams seriously seems to be a return to an era of superstition.

However, what if we were to discover that there were areas in our lives where we already used a similar sort of symbolism and inspiration? This is actually the case, for our dreams have something in common with myths and legends, fairy tales, and indeed, our powers of imagination.

Dreams, fantasy, fairy tales and imagination are lumped together, and our twentieth-century culture, as Robert Johnson says, has developed a prejudice against the imagination.[3]

The lumping together of dreams with fantasy and fairy tales is no accident. All have traditionally served an important purpose in helping people understand themselves. It is only in recent times that fairy tales have been seen as equivalent to children's stories. The great fairy tales were (and are) stories for adults.

The word 'fantasy' has its origins in the Greek word *phantasia*, which means 'to make visible'. Fantasy, fairy tales, imagination and dreams serve the purpose of making visible what is going on inside us — in the inner self.

Virtually every work of art is the product of an imagining mind, yet our derision for fantasy, imaging and dreaming seems to imply that human creativity is actually rational, logical, planned and programmed. How dull!

In fact, very few human advancements, if any, would have originated without imagination and dreams. If human beings had not imagined or dreamed of flying, for example, no energy would have been directed towards its practice. The imagination is an integral part of the conception of ideas.

The use of dreams in literature and the arts affirms the long-standing respect and interest people have for dreams, regardless of the 'science' of the day. Many famous literary works have used dreams as a means to present themes, stories and ideas. They seem to be a universal experience that the reader can relate to — and thus become a powerful literary and visual tool.

Dante's *Divine Comedy* uses a dream as the vehicle for the story, and John Bunyan's *A Pilgrim's Progress* begins as a dream. Some have suggested that Bunyan chose to use the dream motif because it reflected how he was inspired to write the book. Shakespeare makes extensive use of dream sequences in several plays, including *Julius Caesar* and *Richard III*.

In the visual arts, the use of dream motifs is very common. Many artists throughout history have either used dreams as a artistic tool or tried to portray their own dreams. Some notable examples include Colonna's *The Dream of Poliphilo*, Fuseli's *The Nightmare*, Nash's *Landscape of a Dream*, and works by Goya, Blake and many others. Some of the modern schools of painting, such as Dada and Surrealism, used symbols and techniques that were very dream-like, drawing heavily on imagery from the unconscious.

This tradition continued into film. One of the best known presentations of a dream (and some psychoanalysis) occurs in Alfred Hitchcock's *Spellbound*.

A graphic presentation of a dream describing the discomfort the dreamer is unconsciously feeling in waking life is featured in *Babette's Feast*. The unfamiliar and foreign food about to be prepared for a banquet in honour of the father of one of the characters takes on a demonic aspect in the dream, crystallising her fears that the break with tradition, religion, culture and frugality would be against her father's wishes, and her own religious beliefs.

To reject one of our major sources of imagination and fantasy — dreams — is to reject part of our creative spirit, and part of our communion with God, and our inner self.

Dreams and Spirituality

Dreams are a very significant resource for Christians, and for all who are seeking spiritual development. God is interested and involved in our growth as human beings, not just physically or spiritually, but also psychologically. To work on the fountain of material that comes from our unconscious in the form of dreams is to have the opportunity to learn a great deal about ourselves and what makes us tick. It is also work that is significant for others, for the more that we are able to know and love our self, the greater will be our capacity for contribution to others. Relating is clearly part of the activity of God, and so the journey within, and its impact on the outer world, is always a place of potential encounter with God. Encountering and coming to terms with the core of our being can be analogous with developing a relationship with the Divine. (This will be explored in greater depth later.)

Another way of talking about this is to think of it in terms of the explicit and implicit activity of God. Explicit activity could be seen as any direct (yet always interpreted) sense of revelation in a dream or vision. Implicit activity is the presence of the Divine within our self, in part through our being created in the image of God. In this context, God is present in our inner work. Our main focus in this book is on this inner, implicit activity.

Dream interpretation, therefore, is an important resource for those interested in spiritual development and guidance. It can aid our individual development, as the unique person that God has created each of us to be, contributing to our self-awareness, sense of self-esteem, and personhood.

From a religious perspective, dreamwork, and indeed all personal work, aims to create this self-revelation and understanding in addition to being committed to the deepening of our relationship with God. And, as we shall see, the religious life brings with it unique resources in terms of liturgy, prayer and ritual that can help us to externalise our self-discovery.

However, dreamwork from a religious perspective is inadequate if it simply remains at this level. It must also point us to a 'fuller engagement with the continuing ministry of Christ in the world, which is itself the fullness of Christian life as a whole.'[4] It will challenge us to reflect upon our own sense of call and our connection and responsibility to the world around us.

This journey may involve learning (or we should say rediscovering) a new language — the language of symbols and signs that are the script of our unconscious mind (and part of the mind of God). Some of the terms and concepts we will encounter will seem strange, and we may struggle to fit them in with some of our traditional religious language. (For assistance, a glossary of common terms can be found at the back of this book.) When we are in that uncertain state, however, God is often able to speak to us most clearly. The invitation is now to travel on with an open mind, and with an expectation to encounter God in this 'lost world' of dreaming.

For the rediscovery of the importance of dreams, both inside and outside the Christian tradition, we must give thanks to the psychoanalytical school of psychology, and its offspring, analytical psychology. As we will see in subsequent chapters, these approaches take people's inner experiences seriously, and have provided us with an opportunity to re-learn the language of our dreams.

Over the doorway of C. G. Jung's house was an inscription he had found in the writings of the Reformation scholar Erasmus. It read 'Called or not called, the God is present.' It is with that thought we can in confidence enter the land of our dreams.

Notes

1. Jung, C. G. 1989. *Modern Man in Search of a Soul*. London: Routledge. p. 264.
2. Wakefield, G. 1983. *Dictionary of Christian Spirituality*. London: SCM Press.
3. Johnson, R. 1986. *Inner work: Using Dreams and Active Imagination for Personal Growth*. San Francisco: Harper & Row. p. 22.
4. Howe, L. 1986. Dream interpretation in spiritual guidance. *Journal of Pastoral Care*, 40, September. p. 263.

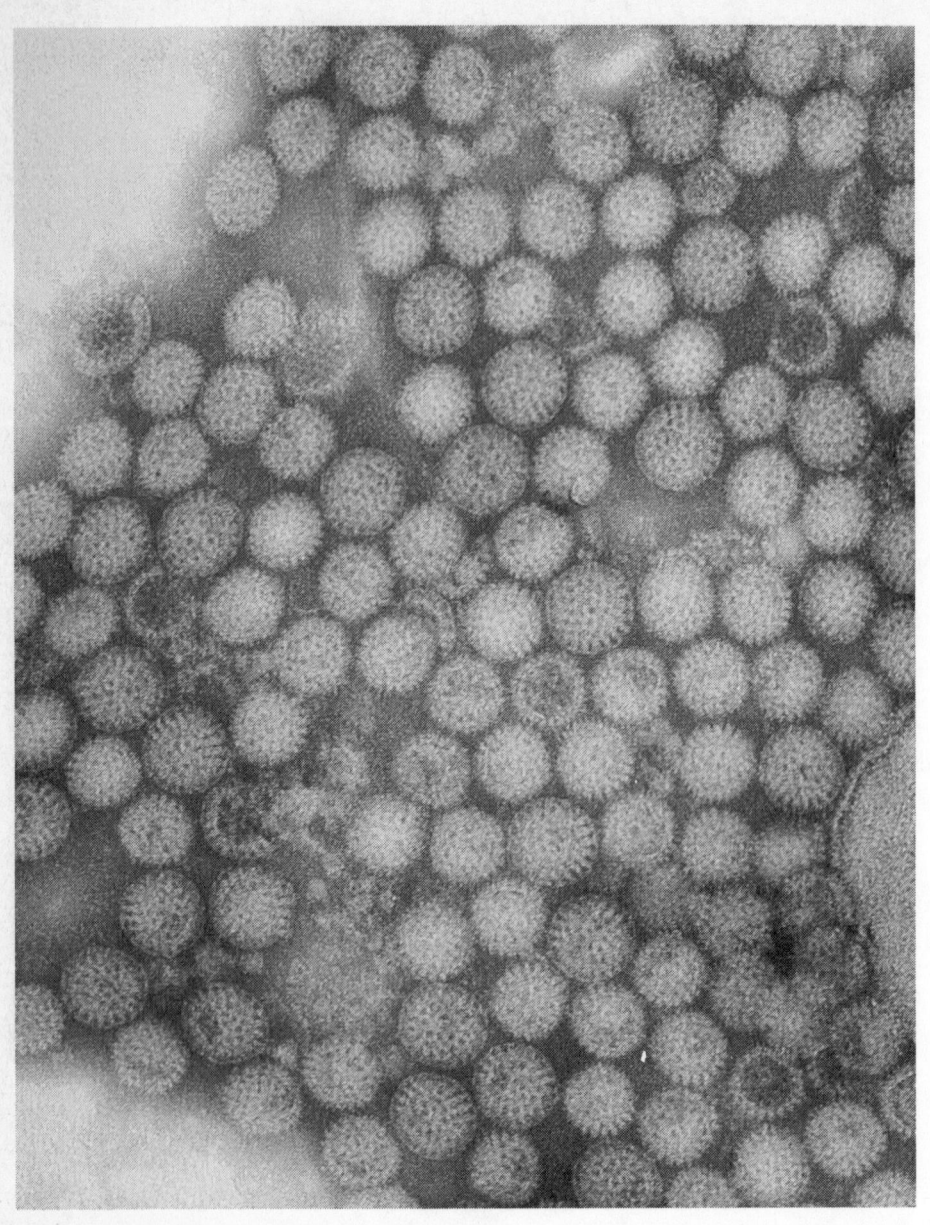
Viral mandala (*Photograph by David Haynes*)

2
DREAM THEORY

Dream *(dri m) n. 1. a. mental activity, usually in the form of an imagined series of events, occurring during certain phases of sleep.*[1]

The Physiology of Dreaming

Ask around and most people will tell you that they dream. Some seem to remember their dreams in remarkable detail, while others are left with an awareness of having dreamt, yet with no recollection of the content of the dream. A few people will state categorically that they never dream. The fact is, everybody dreams, even if not all of us remember our dreams.

Dreaming is an important and necessary part of our sleep. When we are asleep, we move through different levels or cycles of sleep, varying in intensity and depth. Research has shown that dreaming is especially related to what is called REM sleep, REM standing for *rapid eye movement*. In this phase of sleep, which is quite shallow, our eyes begin to move quickly, the body is unable to move, and there is a corresponding change in brain activity. This state is also called 'paradoxical sleep' because it is such a strange and unusual state, with physiological arousal (such as high heart rate), electrical activity in the brain and so on being very close to that of a waking state. Researchers have found that if a person is woken during the REM part of sleep, they tend to remember that they have been dreaming. This is true for people who normally can recall their dreams and for those who say they rarely, if ever, dream. Having discovered that REM sleep and dreams were linked, a variety of other interesting discoveries emerged. If an external stimulus was applied in these periods — for example, the 'guinea pig' being poked with a pin or squirted with a water pistol — these physical actions are often incorporated into the dream.

The inability to move in this state probably accounts to some extent for the common feeling of being trapped, or immobile, in a dream. Our dreaming ego quite correctly perceives the physical impotence of the body, and incorporates it into the dream.

We also know now that events that occur in a dream may be reflected in the brain's physical activity: that, for example, when we dream of a vivid scene, the visual centres of the brain will become active, just as though we were seeing the scene in waking life. We also know that some people can learn to control the events in their dreams (this is called 'lucid dreaming'). Some researchers have been able to arrange with their volunteer subjects to 'go' to certain places in their dreams in a prearranged way. It would seem that the helplessness that most of us experience in our dreams is relatively easy to modify. We can actually have more control of unconscious processes if we are willing to learn.[2]

Further research has shown that if a person is continually woken every time they enter REM sleep, their ability to function when awake declines rapidly. This seems to imply that dreaming is not only something we all do, but is a necessity for psychological health.

Incidentally, these REM periods alter during our lives. A young baby may have six or more hours of REM sleep. This falls to an hour or so in adulthood, and in our later years it may be a half an hour or less.

Obviously, it is not easy to research dreams. Sleep laboratories have tried, for example, to discover whether time in dreams is the same as 'real' time. So far, this sort of research has proved inconclusive, yet it does seem that even for those who clearly remember their dreams, only a part of the time spent dreaming is actually being recalled. We spend far more time in a dream state than we ever are able to recall. Even in a single dream, it seems we at best only recall the tip of the iceberg of the dream, even when we feel the dream has a clear beginning and ending. Whether our conscious mind comes into play and fills in the gaps, or creates a 'capsule' of the dream sequence, we do not know.

Dreams and images may occur in other parts of the sleep cycle, but those occurring in REM sleep are described as having a qualitative difference to these other dreams. They have a more conscious dimension to them, are generally more vivid and include nightmares, but not night terrors (see p. 17).

Lying awake early in the morning, and drifting half in and out of sleep, we may find ourselves in a sort of daydream state, where we are able to construct and control the direction of our dreams to a fair degree. They might be described more as fantasy or story creation — the creative thinking we do to counter-balance a particularly boring week! Such fantasies have their own psychological value and uses.

All of the physiological evidence for dreaming has significance for those who see dreams as an important spiritual or psychological resource. It clearly shows that dreaming is a necessary part of our psychological makeup. If we are denied the capacity to dream, our health will be affected, as will our capacity to function in the 'real' world. Dreams, too, are a natural part of our life — having dreams is not spooky, supernatural or weird. (If anything, perhaps those who seem not to remember their dreams have more to worry about!)

Another implication of research is especially important for those who wish to explore dreams in the context of spirituality. Dreams, it seems, develop within our own psyche. They primarily have their origins within us, rather than in something that originates from outside us. In this sense, dreaming is a resource that helps us learn about ourselves and our attitudes and emotions to the events and experiences we are encountering. While we should note that there is a category of dreams or visions that is more explicitly inspirational, or that may be potentially divine in origin, the majority of dreams we recall are material for and from ourselves. (In the following chapters we will begin to draw a distinction between these two types of experience.)

Dream Reality

Dreams seem to have a reality that is all their own. They are 'real', yet in some way different from our waking reality. Why do we experience these two (or even more) states of reality, and what sort of attention should we pay to 'alternate realities'? Most of us seem to make a distinction between everyday experiences and those we encounter in a dream state, whether during sleep or simply when day-dreaming while gazing out the office window. Yet as far as our minds operate, the emotions and related physiological reactions that are the result of a dream experience are indistinguishable from those that occur in our awake state. We would experience the same emotional feelings when a car attempted to run us down in our dreams as we would if it happened as we were stepping off the footpath in front of our house. Finding ourselves in a boat being tossed about on a stormy sea can evoke the same depth of emotion that we might experience if we were competing in the Sydney to Hobart yacht race. However, it is important to note that in the dream we might find ourselves reacting very differently than we would in real life. We might find ourselves calmly in control, fascinated by the waves, and enjoying the raw energy of the sea in our dream, whereas in reality we might be absolutely petrified! (This difference in our reactions can be a useful point for reflection and analysis.)

Because dream emotion, feelings and responses are in this sense no different from our waking responses, it is not surprising that from time to time people have some difficulty in distinguishing between them. Perhaps you may have experienced something of this difficulty, recalling some past event, perhaps in childhood, and being a little uncertain as to whether it actually happened or was the product of a dream. We are left with a strong sense of its emotional reality, even when its physical manifestation is in question. One client, for example, had a strong early childhood memory of a factory roller door crushing his legs while he was in a pusher. This event never occurred, but the memory was indistinguishable from a real event without verification from family and friends.

The use of certain drugs, medicinal and otherwise, and illness, may trigger dreams, visions and hallucinations, and the question of 'what is real' can then become a concern. An elderly friend was recently admitted to hospital, with a high fever as part of blood poisoning. In her fevered state, she dreamt or hallucinated that she was in a hotel near the seaside. Once she recovered, it was only the insistence of friends and family that convinced her that this excursion had not really occurred. As far as she was concerned, the event was so vivid that she had no way of distinguishing this 'dream state' from actual experience.

These sorts of experiences raise a number of questions for us when we begin to consider the significance of our dreams. For example, the energy and emotion of our dreams is such that we must be extremely cautious of any literalist approach to interpretation. Our senses are easily fooled in terms of our perceptions of reality and we often need external reference points by which to measure our perception of what is happening.

Another issue is perhaps a little more academic. In what ways do illness or chemical stimuli affect our dreaming? Do they 'cause' dreams, or simply stimulate (or over-stimulate) our unconscious? And, as a consequence, are the symbols, language and imagery of dreams in this regard more or less reliable, or different from dream material produced at other times? Some have suggested that the psychic material becomes more primitive or 'raw'. If a person has a strong belief that a dream that occurred in such a state is of consequence and needs to be worked on, then this feeling must be taken seriously. Some psychologists are now suggesting that dreamwork with hospice patients, and those suffering from illness, mental or otherwise, may be extremely helpful to the patient.

Perhaps, in these times of stress or dislocation, we are freed from some of our inhibitions which prevent our paying much attention to our inner life. These experiences confront us with the unconscious dimension of our minds, and demand that it is given attention.

Nightmares and Night Terrors

Nightmare is the common term for any dream that has contents that are both threatening and unusually vivid. Our response to such dreams is one of fear, and many people feel nervous about exploring them. Nightmares, though, are a perfectly normal — in fact universal — type of dream experience. As we will discover, dreams can contain all of our most important and emotionally charged unconscious fantasies, fears and complexes, including emotions that we try to avoid in waking life. It is scarcely surprising that these sometimes erupt with all the fury of overlong containment into our dreams.

Night terrors are something rather different. These almost always occur in children before adolescence. They are characterised by a sudden shriek in the night and a half-awake child who feels terrified, has a racing heart, but who cannot tell her or his parents what is wrong. The child will fall asleep again after ten minutes or so, and have no later memory of the incident. Night terrors occur in the deepest stages of sleep, not in the shallow REM sleep or ordinary dreams (and nightmares). No meaning has ever been found for them; their cause is uncertain, but it seems they eventually cease of their own accord.

Do Dreams Mean Anything?

While scientific research has been able to explore how and where dreaming occurs, it still tells us little about the significance of the content and meaning of dreams.

Many of the explanations proposed by psychologists and psychiatrists this century echo the ideas of previous generations and cultures, although expressed in different language and symbols. For some psychiatrists, dreams are simply the brain winding down at the end of the day, spinning away randomly and out of gear. Ideas, images, emotions appear, a little like the creaks, groans and sighs your car makes as it cools down after a drive. The content is seen to be quite meaningless. Attention is only paid to dreams if they are perceived to be a problem. A recurring dream, or a series of nightmares might fall into this category, as do the well-documented effects of what is called 'post-traumatic disorder syndrome'. This, as the name suggests, is a series of dreams or nightmares that occur after a particularly traumatic event. A person might begin to exhibit these effects after being involved in a plane crash, or having witnessed or been involved in a violent incident. The goal of treatment in these circumstances is generally to remove the disturbing effects, either by therapy or the use of psycho-tropic drugs. Even in this situation, exploration of the dream itself — its content and any potential meaning — may not be seen as important.

Many other psychologists and psychiatrists, however, are beginning to take dreamwork far more seriously, building in particular upon the work of Sigmund Freud, Alfred Adler, Carl Jung and others. Tracing the development of some of their ideas can be helpful in clarifying our own thinking about the nature and meaning of dreams.

We will return to this shortly, but first we will take a look at some of the material from the Judaeo-Christian tradition that refers to dreams.

NOTES

[1] *Collins English Dictionary*, 2nd Australian edn, 1986. Sydney: Collins. p. 465.
[2] Gackenbach, J. & Bosveld, J. 1989. *Control Your Dreams*. New York: Harper Perennial.

Jacob's Dream

And he dreamed, and behold a ladder set up on the earth, and the top of it reached to heaven: and behold the angels of God ascending and descending on it ... (Genesis 28: 12)

3
DREAMS AND THE HEBREW SCRIPTURES

'When we attend to our dreams, we discover that God gives us 'songs in the night.'

(Job 35:10)[1]

Imagine you are part of a group of nomadic people. You awake with a start in the middle of the night, having just had a dream of wolves dressed in armour surrounding your camp. What do you do? In the unlikely event of getting back to sleep, you will most certainly spend time the next day talking about the dream with your companions, and possibly seek out a seer to help you understand the dream and its significance for your tribe — your tribe possibly being any one of a number of ancient peoples, the Hebrews included.

Dreams were universally regarded as an important experience, the property of the community, and a collective interpretation and explanation of them would be sought.

The Dream: Revelation for Community

The Hebrews were no different from any other peoples of antiquity. Dreams were an important part of their cosmology or world view, and were viewed with curiosity, caution and respect. John Priest suggests that there are three main types of dreams in the ancient Middle Eastern tradition, all of which are also encountered in the Hebrew Scriptures.[2] The major type, as we have already mentioned, is a revelation from God. Second, there are dreams that reflect the state of health of the individual. These are uncommon, though perhaps some of the dreams that occur in the story of Job fall into this category. Last, there are dreams that appear to predict a future event. The first and last types of dream are important to the role of the prophet or seer in the Hebrew Scriptures.

Generally, dreams were seen to be a form of divine revelation, and in this respect their source or origin lay outside of the dreamer. They were a way in which a person might be made aware of something, either about themselves, the life situation they found themselves in, or their community, that could not be explained. This leads to two important points about dreaming in the ancient world.

First, because anything as important as a dream would become public property, its retelling, and search for interpretation, affected both the dreamer and the community. This is clearly seen in the use of dreams as part of the prophetic tradition. One of the questions that might first be asked would be 'Is this dream for the community, or the individual?' The answer to that might well depend on the status and reputation of the dreamer; a seer's or prophet's dreams being for all, one of the general populace's just for his or her immediate family circle. It is worth remembering, though, that Hebrew people would not have thought of themselves as individuals in the same way that we might. Even considered as a single entity, their self-understanding was intimately related to the community. When we read stories from another era, we tend to assume that the characters think about themselves in the same way we do. We read back into the story our own self-understanding. In our culture a much greater distinction is drawn between individuals and the community. Because dreams, in ancient times, related primarily to the community, the interpreting of the dream and the spiritual journey itself were always focussed on the welfare, direction, health and wholeness of the community. When we turn to the prophets, we also discover that dreams, as part of the prophetic tradition, became inextricably linked with God's justice-making in the community.

Second, dreams provided a useful literary and story-telling device for convincing others. Thus, when an individual made an important and inexplicable decision, a dream could be invoked to explain it: 'Why did our great great grandfather refuse to go fishing on the day when the sudden storm blew up, when he always went every day without fail ...? Well, my father told me, who was told by his father ... he had a dream ...' and so it goes on. This is not to question the integrity of the Scriptures or any story traditions, but simply to explain how an idea becomes used and represented in literature. The same thing occurs in our own day. For example, there are many stories circulating about people who felt warned in a dream not to catch a certain plane flight, and the plane subsequently crashed. While the warning may not have been real, through the retelling the dream begins to take on more and more significance, and makes the story more compelling and powerful, sometimes well beyond the original event.

When we examine some of the dream stories in the Bible, we should always ask, 'What is the writer trying to convey?' Rarely are they trying to present an argument validating dream interpretation. Rather, the dream is an element in the telling of a more important story.

Early Hebrew Tradition

While the Hebrews shared a dreaming tradition in common with the rest of antiquity, their understanding also came to reflect their own distinctive perspective of the world. As the idea of monotheism developed, so God, rather than a variety of different deities was seen as the source of dreams. Some have suggested, too, that while there are many stories of non-Hebrew dreams in the Old Testament, for example Genesis 20 (Abimelech), Genesis 40 (the story of Joseph and Pharaoh, Daniel etc.), in most cases the correct interpretation for the dream is provided by a Hebrew, often when the local prophets and dream interpreters are unable to decipher the dream. God is seen to aid the true interpretation of dreams.

Many of the symbols present in dreams in the Hebrew Scriptures are shared by other traditions and cultures. For example, eagles, or the vision of an eagle, were associated with power, vision, royalty and God. However, God is rarely encountered in dreams in the Scriptures. Rather, the symbols and imagery become intermediaries for God. This is not surprising, as there was a very strong tradition in Hebrew thought (shared by other religions), that to see God was to die:

> But,' God said, 'you cannot see my face; for no one shall see me and live.(Exodus 33:20)

Dreams might be different from waking reality, but they still had a reality all of their own. A dream encounter with God would be just as destructive as a face-to-face encounter in a waking state.

The Role of the Prophet

A cursory glance through the Hebrew Scriptures will show that many of the references to dreams are in the context of the activity of prophecy. The term 'dreamer of dreams' in Deuteronomy 13:1 is interchangeable with 'prophet' or 'seer'. Dreaming was an accepted part of the prophetic repertoire:

> *And God said, 'Hear my words, when there are prophets among you, I the Lord make myself known to them in visions; I speak to them in dreams.' (Numbers 12:6)*
>
> *When Saul inquired of the LORD, the LORD did not answer him, not by dreams, or by Urim, or by prophets. (1 Samuel 28:6)*

For the early prophets, such as Samuel, dreams were a recognised and credible tool of trade.

The prophet, or seer, dealt not only with their own dreams, but took on the role of 'professional' for others. The kings and queens of antiquity had dream interpreters as part of their court entourage. This is part of Joseph's success in the court of Pharaoh (see Genesis 40). The Hebrew word for 'priest' has its origins in the word 'diviner'.

Certain places also developed a reputation for sacredness. On these, temples and altars were built. Sleeping at one of these special spots made one more likely to receive a revelation in a dream. Jacob has a dream of a ladder reaching from heaven to earth, and, following the experience, declares the place to be holy:

> *Then Jacob woke from his sleep and said, 'Surely the LORD is in this place — and I did not know it!' And he was afraid, and said, 'How awesome is this place! This is none other than the house of God, and this is the gate of heaven.' So Jacob rose early in the morning, and he took the stone that he had put under his head and set it up for a pillar and poured oil on the top of it. He called that place Bethel. (Genesis 28:16–19)*

At another time, God's promise of wisdom to Solomon comes in a dream at Gibeon (1 Kings 3:5).

Dreams that Shape History

Among the most well-known dreams are those in the story of Joseph (Genesis 37 ff.). Dreams play a key role as the story unfolds. Joseph's early dreams of his brothers and family bowing down to him only serve to increase their animosity towards him, leading to his 'unexpected' trip to Egypt. Joseph's ability as a dreamer and interpreter stand him in good stead, allowing him to regain the good favour of Pharaoh. When asked about a dream, Joseph says 'this is what it means...', illustrating that the dream is seen to have a singular meaning. Joseph is quick to remind his colleagues that a word in Pharaoh's ear concerning his own destiny would be appreciated, revealing his own opportunism and possible quest for power. The cultural expectation of a dream needing an 'expert' to interpret it is clearly revealed in these passages, as Joseph's companions are 'gloomy' because they have had dreams and there is no one in the jail to interpret them (Genesis 40:6–8). This has its own risks, as the baker in the story discovers. Having decided that Joseph gives 'favourable interpretations' to dreams, he shares his own, only to be told he will soon be executed (v.16)! When this comes about, Joseph's reputation as an interpreter is validated. Eventually he is returned to Pharaoh's court, this time as an chancellor, on the strength of his ability to unravel Pharaoh's dreams.

At this point, the early dreams of his brothers come into play. In his recognition of them when they come to seek aid in time of famine, Joseph begins to take an active role in the actualising of the dreams. He takes control of the situation, and, in doing so, ensures the fulfilment of the earlier dreams.

The story of Joseph is not primarily about the power of dreams. It serves a far greater purpose in the story of the Hebrews. Yet, it could not but enhance the status of those who were recognised as being able to decipher the strange language of dreams.

There are other ways of looking at these sorts of stories, too. Carl Jung was fascinated by many of these ancient dream episodes, and constructed different psychological interpretations of the dream. For example, they might reveal more about the dreamers' own mental states, and their unconscious awareness of data around them, thus explaining their ability to have a knowledge of what was going on, rather than the dream being an instrument of direct unmediated revelation. From this point of view, Joseph's dream of the wheat bowing before him describes his own innate desire for power, and Pharaoh's dream of the lean years is an unconscious awareness of the changes happening around him that point to the coming of a drought, as part of the natural climatic cycle of the area.

Another dream episode that contains the promise of success, and thereby power, is found in the Book of Judges. Here Gideon overhears the telling of a dream of one of his soldiers, and a discussion about its meaning. The dreamer is told it is a dream of victory for Gideon's army, and so Gideon returns to his own camp, full of confidence, and then initiates a night attack on the Midianites (Judges 7:9–13). In this story the dream sequence is used to reinforce the notion that God is with Gideon, and behind the destiny of the people. Without God's presence, success in battle, or in life, is uncertain.

The powerful story of Job also contains several references to dreams. What is especially interesting here is that they implicitly link the content of dreams to the health of the dreamer. They fall a little more into that category of ancient dreams that reveal the mental, physiological and spiritual condition of the dreamer, rather than the condition of the community (although Job might be seen as a symbol of the community, and its understanding of God). Job, too, explains the purpose of a person's dreams as 'apparitions to turn him from what he is doing, and to put an end to his pride' (Job 33:17).

Edward Edinger notes that this passage also contains the concept of what will later become known as 'compensatory dreaming', where the unconscious turns the dreamer's attention to areas of life that are out of balance, and in need of restructuring.[3]

Yet personal growth and change of the individual are still linked to the life of the community, as all benefit from such growth, just as one person's failings may cause disaster for many.

By the time of the Deuteronomists and the later prophets, there are a number of warnings appearing about false dreams and those who interpret them. A clear warning is given in Deuteronomy 13:

If prophets or those who divine by dreams appear among you and promise you omens or portents, and the omens or the portents declared by them take place, and they say, 'Let us follow other gods (whom you have not known) and let us serve them', you must not heed the words of those prophets or those who divine by dreams; for the LORD your God is testing you, to know whether you indeed love the LORD your God with all your heart and soul.

This is an especially interesting passage, for the interpretation of a dream is judged as to whether or not it enhances the religious life and the worship of God. If it is against the religious and social ethic, then it is to be rejected, unless it leads to challenging and changing traditional patterns of behaviour, both for the individual and the community. Its focus is always to be life-enhancing for all, not anarchistic or nihilistic. This provides a fairly sound basis for working with any dream in our own setting.

We could say that we have here an 'ethic of dreaming'. This 'ethic' is equally applicable when considering 'dream' in the meaning of a plan, idea or proposal we may have. Are our personal plans life-enhancing for all, or simply for ourselves?

The passage above also presents us with an illustration of how dreams were interpreted. The dream as revelation is normally symbolic in language, yet is seen to have only one meaning. The dream (and its interpretation) is either true or false. In later chapters we will have the opportunity to compare this approach to the contemporary psychological models, where a dream may have a multiplicity of meanings, and may evolve over time, perhaps as part of a dream series, or simply upon further reflection and contemplation.

The book of Jeremiah also presents a scepticism and warning about dreams and their potential for misdirection. Jeremiah rails against the false prophets of the day:

I have heard what the prophets have said who prophesy lies in my name, saying, 'I have dreamed, I have dreamed!' How long? Will the hearts of the prophets ever turn back — those who prophesy lies, and who prophesy the deceit of their own heart? They plan to make my people forget my name by their dreams that they tell one another, just as their ancestors forgot my name for Baal. Let the prophet who has a dream tell the dream, but let the one who has my word speak my word faithfully. What has straw in common with wheat? says the LORD. Is not my word like fire, says the LORD, and like a hammer that breaks a rock in pieces? See, therefore, I am against the prophets, says the LORD, who steal my words from one another. See, I am against the prophets, says the LORD, who use their own tongues and say, 'Says the LORD.' See, I am against those who prophesy lying dreams, says the LORD, and who tell them, and who lead my people astray by their lies and their recklessness, when I did not send them or appoint them; so they do not profit this people at all, says the LORD. (Jeremiah 23)

Dreams are becoming a source of suspicion, the true prophet's word coming from the one who 'speaks' faithfully. The integrity of the prophet is called into question, the ability to 'prophesy' in whatever manner is no longer a guarantee of trustworthiness.

Dreams do not fall totally into disrepute, although there no longer seems to be the unquestioning acceptance of their role as a primary prophetic tool. As we approach the inter-testamental period, they experience a resurgence, particularly in some of the popular writings and stories. The story of Daniel is an excellent example of this.

The book of Daniel is a late addition to the Hebrew Scriptures. Written around 165 BC, its aim was to present a story, placed in an earlier time, that would inspire faith and hope among a community that was suffering persecution at the hands of Antiochus Epiphanes. With its future focus in the latter chapters, and full of visions and symbols, this type of literature is called 'apocalyptic' writing, and is similar to the Book of Revelation in the New Testament.

In a scene reminiscent of Joseph, Daniel, the hero, is able to interpret Nebuchadnezzar's dream. This dream has caused such distress that the king is no longer able to sleep. Where the other diviners fail, Daniel, having discovered the king's dream and its meaning in a dream of his own, succeeds. From here on, a succession of dreams is presented, some from the king, others from Daniel. The dreams are a literary device, for within them they contain the hidden messages that were to explain to the readers what was happening in their own day. It is a fascinating book in its own right, but for our purposes we will limit ourselves to what it tells us about the status of dreams. In Daniel, the older idea of dream as revelation, in need of interpretation, and with one meaning, is evident. It is coupled with the idea of a prophetic and futuristic element to some dreams. They are not simply describing what is, but what will be. Even in its most cautious evaluation, the presentation of the dreams in Daniel must have reinforced and validated the popular view of dreams as auguries of the future.

Dream or Vision?

References to dreams in both the Hebrew Scriptures and the New Testament are often associated with 'visions'. 'Visions', in fact, appears to be the more popular term used by New Testament times. In many passages the words dream and vision are used interchangeably, probably as part of the literary style. After all, it becomes a bit boring to use the same word over and over again!

Jacob is spoken to in a dream (Genesis 28) and in a 'vision of the night' (Genesis 46). The same expressions appear in Job (Job 20:8; 33:15), Isaiah (Isaiah 29:7) and Daniel (Daniel 2:19). The phrase 'visions of the night' seems to describe the dream as something that happens as part of sleep, and as a subset of a vision. A vision, on the other hand, might be used to describe an experience that occurred in a state of prayer or in a trance (Acts 11:5). The Greek word for dream in the New Testament derives from the idea of 'something presented during sleep' — a 'sleep vision'. A dream could be seen to be a specific form of vision. In either case, however, the dream or vision is given to bring a change in direction and to encourage alignment with God's purpose.

As we turn to the New Testament, we will see something of this gradual change both in terminology and understanding of dreaming.

Notes

[1] Keen, S. 1994. *Hymns to an Unknown God: Awakening the Spirit in Everyday Life*. New York: Bantam. p. 264.
[2] Priest, J. 1990. Myths and dreams in the Hebrew scriptures. In J. Campbell (ed.), *Myth, Dreams and Religion*. Dallas: Spring.
[3] Edinger, E. 1986. *Encounter with the Self*. Toronto: Inner City. p. 47.

The Temptation of St. Anthony

4
DREAMS AND THE CHRISTIAN ERA

In the last days it will be, God declares, that I will pour out my Spirit upon all flesh, and your sons and daughters shall prophesy, and your young men shall see visions, and your old men shall dream dreams.

(Acts 2:17)

Dreams and the New Testament

In the New Testament, the occurrence of dreams becomes rarer, or perhaps we should say more selective.

One of the major references to dreams comes as part of the birth narratives. Joseph has several dreams, each of which causes a change in direction. He is spoken to by an angel in a dream, which causes him to change his mind and remain with Mary (Matthew 1:20). The appearance of an angel emphasises the dream as a vehicle for a message from God. Again, the idea of the dream as an intermediary between God and the person is present.

Joseph and Mary's major movements are all dream initiated. They flee to Egypt after a warning in a dream (Matthew 2:13), and finally the return to Israel, specifically Galilee, is initiated by another dream (Matthew 2:20; 2:22).

These dreams of revelation in Matthew affirm God's presence, and God's guidance. By using dreams, Matthew is saying, 'This did not happen by accident, but is part of the design of God, and is part of the future unfolding.' Myth, and dreams, in the Christian Scriptures, are shaped by this 'eschatological consciousness'.

With the exception of Joseph's first dream, all of the dreams in the gospel of Matthew are warnings. The 'wise ones' are told in a dream not to return to Herod (having already done most of the damage!):

> *But they were given a warning in a dream not to go back to Herod, and returned to their country by a different way. (Matthew 2:20)*

As part of the trial of Jesus, Pilate is warned by his wife:

> *While he was sitting on the judgment seat, his wife sent word to him, 'Have nothing to do with that innocent man, for today I have suffered a great deal because of a dream about him'. (Matthew 27:19)*

Unfortunately, the message goes unheeded, and Pilate, despite 'washing his hands' of the affair, will come to be associated throughout history with the death of Jesus. Thus, we have another warning dream, but it is one that is neglected and in a sense unfulfilled.

Probably the most well-known reference to dreams in the New Testament is to be found in the book of Acts, in chapter two:

> *In the last days it will be, God declares, that I will pour out my Spirit upon all flesh, and your sons and your daughters shall prophesy, and your young men shall see visions, and your old men shall dream dreams. (Acts 2:17)*

This is a quote from Joel 2:28, linked in Acts to the outpouring of the Spirit. Dreams, then, become part of the activity of the Holy Spirit. Despite this affirmation, however, there are few references to dreams from here on. We continue to encounter a preference for the term 'vision', which is used to cover a variety of supernatural experiences.

There are a number of possible explanations for this. First, with the Gospel message centred in the person of Jesus there was little necessity for it to be centred in dreams as the prime mediator of the presence of God. 'No New Testament witness thought of basing the central message, the Gospel, or any essential part of it, as dreams,' Amos Wilder reminds us.[1]

Second, the Jewish and early Christian communities were in a state of flux, influenced by traditional Jewish culture as well as Greek and Roman philosophy. In such an environment, the term 'vision' may have been more acceptable.

Third, a dream was open to interpretation, whereas a vision, it seems, was perceived to be far more immediate in its manifestation, and less liable to be misunderstood. A good example of this is Cornelius' 'dream' in Acts 10:3:

> *One afternoon at about three o'clock he had a vision in which he clearly saw an angel of God coming in and saying to him, 'Cornelius ...'.*

The implicit comment about the time of day seems to be implying, 'Hey! I wasn't dreaming! This was for real!' A dream might be misinterpreted or could lead one astray, but a vision in the daytime was something trustworthy, and far less ephemeral. Peter's associated revelation occurs not in a dream, but in a trance as part of his midday prayers (Acts 10:10).

Someone might want to ask at this point, 'What about the Book of Revelation?' The Book of Revelation has been a continual source of contention and confusion within the church for centuries. Although some of the imagery is very 'dream-like' in character, it is actually presented as a vision, the product of an ecstatic experience (Revelation 1:10), and is what is called apocalyptic literature, rather like the book of Daniel.[2]

Another change in the perception of dreams can be discovered in the book of Ecclesiasticus (Ben Sira). Written around 150–200 BC, it is part of what is called the deutero-canonical books, and has re-appeared in most recent Bibles, such as the Jerusalem Bible. It speaks against the growing Hellenisation of the Palestinian community. Here we find a statement about dreams that is almost a forerunner to a modern or psychological view of the dream:

Vain and deceptive hopes are for the foolish, and dreams lend wings to fools. As well clutch at shadows and chase the wind as put any faith in dreams. Dreams are no different from mirrors; confronting a face, the reflection of that face ... Divinations, dreams and auguries are nonsense, like the fantasies of a pregnant woman. Unless sent as emissaries from the Most High, do not give them a thought; for dreams have led many astray, and those who relied on them have come to grief. Fulfilling the Law requires no such falsehood, and wisdom is perfected in veracity. (Ecclesiasticus 34:1–8)

Again, there is a clearly stated scepticism about the role of dreams as a spiritual or guiding tool. This is probably written as polemic against many of the common practices of the day, especially those that were a part of Hellenistic culture. It reveals the common fascination with dreams and other means of divination people sought in the same way that people use astrology, tarot, tea leaves and long-range economic forecasts today.

The phrase 'dreams are no different from mirrors' is especially interesting, implying that what is encountered in the dream is a product, and reflection, of the self in most cases. This is far removed from the understanding of dreams we encountered in Genesis.

There are dreams, the quote above states, that do come from 'the Most

High', and these are important. Unfortunately, it does not offer any guidance as to how one is to tell the two apart!

The Early Christian Communities

In the early Christian church, dreams feature regularly, but again not without some degree of caution. This attitude is also reflected in the Jewish literature of the period. As Christianity sprang from this tradition, one could assume that some of its ideas regarding dreams, at least at a popular level, would be shared.

In the Talmud, there are sections devoted to dreams and their interpretation, and these provide a window into the popular thought of the time:

> *Although I (God) have hidden my face from Israel, I will communicate with him through dreams. (Chag. 5b)*

Having had a dream that was not understood, a person was instructed to take it to the priests, and pray for enlightenment.

Reference is made to three types of dreams that are 'fulfilled', or especially significant — morning dreams, a dream where the dreamer is accompanied by a companion or friend, and a dream that is interpreted in a dream. Therapists today would generally consider each of these dreams as being worthy of attention.

Scriptural texts were used to aid the interpretation of dreams. For example, dreaming of a well was a sign of peace because of a verse in Genesis, where Isaac's servants dug, and found 'wells of living water' (Genesis 26:19).

There is an interesting occurrence of 'inversion', also found in other religious traditions, where a dream of something normally seen as 'negative' is a sign of something good. Dreaming of a corpse in one's house, for example, is a sign of peace in the home! This reappears much later in the work of Jung and others, called 'compensatory' or 'complementary' dreaming. The unconscious contains all the unused, untapped and shadow elements of a person, which commonly appear in dreams. From this perspective, a religious person should regularly have pagan dreams, and an atheist religious dreams! Both would find this somewhat disturbing.

Dreams were also believed to be a means of communication with the dead. This idea was shared with other cultures, too, for example, in African tribal religion, and continued into some expressions of Christianity.[3]

The Talmud also contains the story of a Rabbi who took the same dream he had to twenty-four interpreters. All gave different interpretations, yet, he says, all came to be realised in him. There is a comment after this story that suggests this is evidence of the Divine at work in the interpreters. In such a story we see the idea that the value of the dream lay not so much with the dreamer, but with the interpreter, a product of the older concept that dreams were community property. We may also conclude that the act of examination and reflection becomes part of the healing or insight process, beyond the actual content of the dream.

The role of the interpreter has been mentioned previously. Carl Jung posed some interesting questions about the interpreter of dreams, which are equally applicable to the ancient tradition of diviner and the modern 'analyst' or 'therapist'. Who dominates in the discussion of the dream — the dreamer or the interpreter? If it is the latter, the interpretation will no doubt tell us more about the analyst than it does about the dreamer.[4] For this reason, among others, Jung held a strong belief that only the dreamer could truly comprehend his or her own dream.

The Evolution of Christian Thought about Dreams

The Christian tradition is never revealed as one unchanging set of beliefs and values. Within the tradition, there have been times of great diversity and variety. In the early church, we can assume that many of the ideas we encountered in Judaism and Greek and Roman culture were popular. While we have many records of the thoughts of the early church leaders, we can only speculate as to how ordinary people thought and acted.

The Hebrew tradition, which had a relatively wholistic view of the person — with little separation of the mind and the body — was the crucible from which the Christian tradition emerged. Body and mind could not be separated or exist independently. But the early Christians were also heavily influenced by Hellenism and the streams of Greek philosophy that it contained. Greek thought brought with it the idea of separate elements of the person — body, mind and spirit (or soul). Here the 'soul', had an independence from the body.

These concepts came to be accepted as the normal understanding for Christian thought throughout the following centuries. Even today, a great deal of Christian theology, especially at a populist level, is based on a Greek idea of the person, which is used to re-interpret the Biblical texts.

This diversity is reflected in the difficulties early Christian writers had when they encountered dreams. On one hand, they were quick to recognise dreams' long tradition in the Scriptures, and their role as a 'message' from God, but at the same time the enormous number of dreams people had meant that not all these dreams could be classified as divine communications, especially when some dreams seemed to contain very 'unChristian' imagery. Therefore, their attention was drawn to trying to sort out which dreams were true or false, which were of religious value and which were not.

This effort produced many different ideas about the nature of dreams, some of them quite advanced. Tertullian saw dreams as a form of activity the soul adopted while the body was at rest, and as akin to death. Clement took this idea further, suggesting that in this state the soul was more able to reflect upon itself, and that true dreams revealed the relationship between the dreamer and God. This is quite an advanced notion. The dream is becoming the product of the dreamer's own psyche (albeit with the inspiration of God), and reveals material about the person.

Gregory of Nyssa took a different path. He identified some dreams, such as the Biblical dreams of Joseph and Daniel, as dreams inspired or created by God. They were perhaps not so much dreams as visions. The normal everyday sort of dreams, on the other hand, were the product of the body, for example, being caused by digestion and containing images from waking life. The dream could also reveal something of the person's character, whether he or she was peaceful, angry and upset, and so forth.

St Augustine seemed to accept that dreams could be the inspiration of the Divine. Indeed, he recalled that his mother had a dream of his own conversion.

Thomas Aquinas also believed dreams were inspired and could be prophetic, but he was equally concerned with the problem of the truth or falsity of such phenomena. He developed a concept where some dreams came from within, either from the soul or the body, and other dreams from God, or alternatively from demons. Aquinas, then, sought to cover all possibilities!

In the second century AD, the philosopher Artemidorus wrote a book entitled *Oneirocritica* (The Interpretation of Dreams), containing advice and guidance for dream interpretation. This book continued to be reprinted and circulated widely, even in Luther's time. In addition, throughout all these periods of history, there were a great number of dream books that catalogued dreams, describing their meaning. These books were immensely popular and widely read. The general public were saying 'tell us more' (especially about the more lascivious bits!).

The use of dreams in literature and the arts also illustrates their wide appeal and acceptance (see also references to dreams and art).

As a historical footnote, we may also recall that the dominance of Christianity itself is reputedly owed to a dream. Constantine dreamt of a cross just before a major battle, and, crediting his victory to the presence of the Christian God, converted to Christianity, bringing with him the whole Roman Empire.

The Loss of a Dreamwork Tradition

The diversity of viewpoints above did little to counteract the demise of a dreamwork tradition, and indeed contributed to it. In such a confusing environment, it would take only three things to tip the scale towards a condemnation at worst, and suspicion at the least, of dream interpretation.

The first of these things was brought about by the scholar Jerome. In his early life, Jerome had made use of the spiritual resources of dreaming, but when he prepared the Latin translation of the Bible (the Vulgate), it appears he deliberately mistranslated a key word in the text. The Hebrew word for witchcraft or soothsaying is *anan*. On three occasions (including Leviticus 19:26 and Deuteronomy 18:10), the word was translated not as 'witchcraft and soothsaying' but as 'augury nor observing dreams.'[5] The Vulgate would become the basis for virtually all translations of the Bible until the twentieth century, and would from here on contain a prohibition against dream interpretation.

No clear reason emerges as to why Jerome took such action. Was it a personal view in later life, at odds with his earlier experience, pressure from the church hierarchy, or concern at the 'fortune telling' style of dreamwork that was popular in his day?

Certainly the use of dreams as a form of prediction or fortune telling was of concern to the church's scholars and leaders. This became another reason for the decline in dream interpretation. This form of dreamwork was far removed from its practice as a spiritual discipline. For the church in the West, dreamwork would become a casualty in the fight against increasing magic and superstition that arrived with the barbarian invasions.

With the rediscovery of Aristotelian philosophy in the eleventh century, the dreamwork tradition was further marginalised. As noted earlier, Aquinas had a somewhat eclectic view of dreams, but in his attempts to modernise Christianity within an Aristotelian framework, dreams were given little if any value. Reality was to be experienced by the senses, and by rational thought, and there was little place for dreams other than the fact that they occurred.

Jerome's version of the Bible, the battles against increasing superstition and magic, and finally the rise of rationalism served to remove dreamwork from the agenda of mainstream spiritual disciplines.

The Rise of Rationalism and the Decline of the Dream

The ideas above continued to dominate European Christianity over the next centuries. Dreams were indeed mysterious and the symbols in dreams seemed to bear an increasing relationship to the darker side of life rather than the divine. By the Enlightenment, dreams had become associated with demons and evil, the dreamer being in the grip of the powers of darkness.

This identification of dreams as a part of the dark side of life continued to influence their growing neglect. This was then reinforced from a different direction with the rise of rationalism. Whereas the Hebrew world viewed the spiritual and physical as a unity, and the Greek-influenced Christian world as a duality, rationalism would simply ignore the 'spiritual' side. This left a world that was primarily physical, and where meaning and value were ascribed on the basis of function.

The new ideas of rationalism, humanism, and 'hard' science placed humanity at the centre of the universe in a way that previous philosophies had not. With a new centrepoint, ideas about reality needed review, and thinkers such as Descartes and Pascal, for example, debated how we might know something is 'real', and what the difference is between our waking life and that of our dreams. The dream's content became the product of body function, its source internal and its meaning irrelevant. Robert Burton wrote, 'The gods send not our dreams, we make our own.'[6]

By the end of the nineteenth century, rationalism had not banished the dream, but had made it a product of curiosity and amusement, with little power. Empirically, there was indisputable evidence for dreams, and discussion centred around providing reasons for their occurrence in terms of the biological and neurological functions of the body. Some attention also began to be paid to dreams in the treatment of the mentally ill, and it is from this environment that the ideas of Freud, Jung and others would spring.

In terms of credibility, this brought with it an unfortunate legacy, as the dreams of ordinary 'normal' people were overlooked. A rationalist approach to mental illness might concede that dreams were a feature of a problem, but they would be a symptom to be treated (that is, removed) rather than something that had any meaning or purpose beyond a physiological or neurological phenomenon. Dreams might be a factor for the ill, but little was said about the normality of dreaming until Jung. We still encounter the remnants of this association with mental illness today, when we are reticent to share a dream with someone, because we think they will see us as 'crazy' or 'out of our mind'. In fact, with dreams, we are well and truly 'in our mind'!

A Bigger Picture

This chapter has mainly focussed on dreaming within Western Christianity and a European tradition. Most other cultures had a high regard for dreams, often ascribing not just religious value but what we would call psychological value to the experience. (Chinese philosophy is an example of this.) John Mbiti notes the practice of dream interpretation in African religions, and the manner in which these traditions become incorporated into various expressions of Christianity.[7]

In Australia, there is an immensely rich tradition of dreaming in Aboriginal culture, and we who have been brought up on a diet of Western expressions of Christianity (whether from Europe or America) have much to learn from our Aboriginal sisters and brothers.

Notes

[1.] Wilder, A. 1990. Myth and dream in Christian scripture. In J. Campbell (ed.), *Myth, Dream and Religion*. Dallas: Spring. p. 70.
[2.] Although generally considered apocalyptic literature, some recent scholars, such as Elizabeth Schlüsser Fiorenza, have created new interest in the book, suggesting that it is primarily pastoral rather than apocalyptic. Unfortunately, the reputation of Revelation has been damaged by those who have approached it in a very literal sense, offering 'prophetic' interpretations, and discrediting both the Scripture, to say nothing of the damage wrought upon their readers.
[3.] Mbiti, J. 1970. *Concepts of God in Africa*. London: SPCK. p. 267.
[4.] Jung, C. 1964. *Man and His Symbols*. London: Aldus. p. 57–8.
[5.] Kelsey, M. 1991. *God, Dreams and Revelation*. Minneapolis: Augsburg (Fortress). p. 159.
[6.] Mackenzie, N. 1965. *Dreams and Dreaming*. London: Aldus. p. 81.
[7.] Mbiti, J. 1970. *Concepts of God in Africa*. London: SPCK.

Jung Country *(Photo by David Haynes)*

5
THE EARLY PSYCHOLOGISTS

The phenomenology of the psyche is so colourful, so variegated in form and meaning that we cannot possibly reflect all its riches in one mirror.

Carl Jung[1]

The Legacy of Freud, Jung and the Early Psychologists

While most academic psychologists (and most introductory psychology books) have little or nothing to say about dreams, a few researchers and psychotherapists have made major contributions to knowledge in this area. In so doing, they have renewed the old thread of traditional dream interpretation and added to this a great deal of information from objective and detailed observation of dream imagery. Basically, there have been two sources of this information: sleep laboratories and the findings of therapists who work with their clients' dreams.

As we have seen in chapter two, sleep laboratories have told us a lot about dreaming as a physical brain activity, although relatively little about the content and meaning of dreams. We have learnt that the earliest dreams in a night seem to be those that most resemble waking thoughts and that, as the night goes on, earlier and earlier memories and more vivid imagery begin to appear. The great majority of dream images involve the presence of other people — most dreams are social, or collective, in other words. Yet most dreams from sleep laboratories have proved to be rather dull and matter of fact. They are brief, and often feature the sleep laboratory itself. When more dramatic themes are present, they often contain themes such as being imprisoned in a time capsule by alien beings in white coats!

All this reflects the observations of many psychotherapists. The dreams we remember are those that have the most relevance to our immediate life needs. If we are in the rather unusual and uncomfortable situation of a sleep laboratory, then the laboratory, and our anxieties about it, will be featured in our dreams. Similarly, if we enter psychotherapy, the dreams that are remembered are very likely to reflect the unconscious problems that brought us there in the first place. The unconscious is often more 'co-operative' than we give it credit for. In the sleep laboratory, it will give us dreams about spaceships and mad scientists, in Freudian therapy it may well produce sexual dream themes, and in Jungian therapy it is very likely to produce themes of spiritual conflict or development.

It is the practising psychotherapists who have been most able to tell us how we can understand the mass of material that dreams throw up. Sigmund Freud, Alfred Adler and Carl Jung laid the foundations upon which others would build.

Sigmund Freud

No name is as well identified with study of the mind for most people than that of Sigmund Freud (1856–1939). Words and expressions such as 'Freudian', 'Freudian slip' and 'word association' have entered common usage, even if their meaning is not fully understood. Exploring the role of dreams was central to the development of Freud's psychoanalytical theory, as, in his own words, dream analysis was the 'royal road to the unconscious'.

In 1899, he published a book, *The Interpretation of Dreams*, where he began to explain his psychological theory.[2]

In very simple terms, Freud saw people as driven by needs, desires and wishes. Many of these drives were hidden or suppressed in the unconscious part of the mind, and energy was used to keep them hidden from the conscious part of the mind. Dream interpretation, word association and word 'slips' (which became known as Freudian slips) could reveal something of the suppressed drives, which were unacceptable to a conscious mind educated by parental influence and the world around it.

Freud was one of the first to take seriously the idea of an unconscious part of the mind. In his clinical work, he observed a variety of psychological conditions such as obsessions, hallucinations, phobias and delusions, which he concluded were the result of defence mechanisms in the mind attempting to ward off hidden, unpleasant or unacceptable feelings and emotions. Using the practice of free association, he found that many of his patients would begin to talk about their dreams. (Free association was a process where beginning with an image, the client would say the first thing that came into his or her head, then the next, then the next and so on until a chain of associations related to the original image was produced.) In addition to this clinical experience, Freud sought to have some understanding of his own dreams.

Freud also described how dreams often show 'condensation' — the ability to put together, in a single dream, a whole collection of ideas and images from different times and areas of one's life. This is because all these ideas and images are bound together by a particular theme — often a theme closely linked to a particular feeling — that the unconscious mind considers to be important. Perhaps a whole series of 'unrelated' events from childhood onwards — a tea party, a bicycle ride, a wedding, a Saturday night dance, a holiday — were all actually linked to, for example, feelings of jealousy that had long been forgotten. If the emotional link of a series of condensed images of this sort could be found, we might discover one of our life-themes and understand that, emotionally or behaviourally, there is more continuity in our life than we imagined.

Freud also described how dreams may have both an overt ('manifest') and a covert ('latent') content. They are not always what they seem, in other words (or, in a more complicated way, they may be both what they appear to be on the surface *and* something else at the same time). A dream about yesterday's events may be both a literal memory of these events and a symbolic re-enactment (or re-experiencing) of events from earlier in life that have the same sort of feelings or meanings for us. Thus, a dream about yesterday's veterans rugby match may also be a symbolic re-experiencing of being bullied at school thirty years ago, for example. That's why, in the dream, instead of enjoying the match, we feel afraid and tearful.

Dreams, said Freud, were symbolic in nature. That is, the image in a dream stood for something else. The image of a person standing in the middle of a hot desert might signify, for example, that they were 'hot-blooded'.

Dreams, then, basically became a way of encountering the suppressed material in the unconscious. For Freud, much of this material was shaped in childhood. The predominant drive was sexual, although he would later suggest that a drive to aggression and self-destruction might be almost as significant. (Interestingly, this observation emerged during a time when he struggled with depression.)

When one considers the period in which Freud lived, with its strict morality, and the cross-section of patients he worked with (virtually all suffering from psychological problems), it is not surprising that he came to see the sex drive as the key cause of mental dysfunction. The suppression of this drive, caused by conflict between the conscious and unconscious mind (later to be termed the 'ego' and the 'id') was seen to lead to anxiety, neurosis and illness. Within this structure, most of the symbols that emerged in dreams were sexual.

However, in the Freudian model, the symbols tended to be one-dimensional, and defined by the drive behind them. For example, a sword would clearly be seen as a phallic symbol, a cave or open doorway a symbol of female genitalia. This can be described as a reductionist model of dream interpretation, because of the singular meaning ascribed to the symbols.

Dreams for Freud were attempts to fulfil a wish — created by the instinctual drives — and therefore often contained imagery or suggestions of behaviour that the dreamer would normally deny or reject:

The fulfilment of a wish is its [the dreams] only purpose ... the dream therefore is the disguised fulfilment of a (suppressed, repressed) wish.[3]

While dreams might be wish fulfilment, they also existed to conceal, rather than reveal, the instinctual drives of the unconscious. They served as 'guardians of sleep'. It was easier for the mind to deal with, disguise or control the primitive urges by dispelling their energy through dreams, thus protecting the conscious mind in its rest state and prolonging sleep.

However, Freud's point that dreams may actually represent wishes and thoughts that would be rejected by consciousness is an important one. It introduces the principle of 'compensation' — the way that dreams (and other manifestations of the unconscious) are so often representations of those aspects of ourselves that we deny or are unwilling to examine. It is as though, if we repress or avoid any important aspect of ourselves, the material involved will be most reluctant to be confined to the unconscious and will bubble up in our dreams until it gains our attention.

Another of Freud's valuable contributions to dreamwork was the notion of 'secondary revision'. This described the tendency for the conscious part of the mind to re-order or reconstruct a dream when retold, especially on a second or third retelling. The same observation could be made when we compare the verbal retelling of a dream to the way we might write it out in a journal. Freud assumed that the parts of the story that 'dropped' out related to disturbing or sensitive material. Whether the omissions are unintentional or deliberate, conscious or unconscious, most analysts would agree with Freud that attention paid to these discrepancies or omissions can be particularly fruitful.

Freud described very well the sorts of symbols that we see in dreams, but his analyses had two major limitations. He maintained (against all the evidence) that all important dreams are based on sexual and aggressive urges, and that spiritual and many other needs are simply disguised versions of these urges. In such a framework, he ignored spiritual dreams, and any concept of spirituality. This, to many people, is so great a limitation as to make his whole approach to dream analysis very limited and not very interesting.

Freud also believed that dreams are couched in symbolic language in order to *disguise* their true meanings. There is a deliberate attempt by the unconscious to prevent the dreamer from consciously understanding what the dream means (because the latter actually represents unacceptable sexual and aggressive wishes). This would seem to impute conscious purpose to the unconscious mind, dooming us to being forever haunted by anxiety-provoking dreams that we must not understand, and is an over-negative and restrictive approach.

Another of the criticisms levelled at Freud's work is that it was developed in a clinical setting, mainly from his experience with patients who were mentally ill. Little work was done on 'normal' people. This bias created a scenario where everyone was seen to be, to a greater or lesser extent, in psychological conflict. Additionally, the psychoanalytic model, as do all theories, reflected the life and experience of its creator. As a Jew, a rebel and a radical thinker operating outside the elitist medical establishment in Vienna, Freud experienced rejection and was often in conflict with his peers. Therefore, it is not surprising to find that the Freudian model is basically a model of psychological conflict and suppression.

Even with these limitations in mind, Freud's contribution cannot be understated. He underscored the concept that dreams were an important psychological resource and that all dream material had a meaning.

It is paradoxical that orthodox Christianity, with its emphasis on sin and the fallenness of humanity, did not take more comfort from Freudian-based conflict models. In some ways some of these models echo one interpretation of Paul when he wrote:

I do not understand my own behaviour. I do not as I mean to ... every time I do what I do not want to, then it is not myself acting, but the sin that lives in me ... (Romans 7:14a ff.)

However, for the conservative society and religion of the day, Freud appeared to be unleashing the very 'evil' drives that socialisation had sought to bury.

Freud had gathered around him a group of colleagues, calling themselves psychoanalysts. Even in its early days, rifts began to appear within this circle. Several of Freud's colleagues found themselves disagreeing with some of the fundamental presuppositions of the Freudian model.

Alfred Adler

In 1911, Alfred Adler was one of the first to make a break with Freud. Rather than sex, Adler thought power and superiority were the key instinctual drives. People suffered a sense of inferiority when their inner 'lifestyle' did not mesh with reality.

From Adler comes the concept that dreams are, sometimes, the continuation of waking thought processes — only confusing because they are seen in symbolic language. Adler, and Adlerian psychologists, have given many examples of dream-thoughts of this kind. One of the most famous of these is the story of Kekule and the discovery of the benzene ring (see chapter six). Many of us may have experienced the situation where we are haunted by an apparently insoluble problem, go to bed, and awake with the solution all ready for us in the morning.

Adler also introduced the important idea that 'The purpose of dreams must be in the feelings they arouse (and leave) behind.'[4] It is very important when analysing dreams to bear in mind that logical thought is a very minor aspect of unconscious functioning and that the essence of understanding the great majority of dreams lies in intuitive understanding of the feeling pattern present. People who value logic and systematic thought especially need to bear this in mind. If we begin with the assumption that our most important dreams will represent those aspects of our mind that we habitually overlook, fear or dislike, and that they are presented in feeling and intuitive form, we will have made a good beginning.

Adler, as a socialist, wished to encourage persons to reach their full potential and be able to participate in society. This was the ultimate goal of therapy and personal development.

Such caution is worth underlining in the context of spirituality, also. Does our wish to grow spiritually emanate simply from a desire to improve ourselves, or does it have an outward focus — to equip us to fully participate in our community — as Adler was suggesting?

Maeder, a colleague of Adler's, would take some of these ideas further, describing dreams as exercises that prepared us for waking life. In later times, others would pick up this idea and continue its development.

Further Developments

After the First World War, many soldiers suffered from recurring nightmares. Among those working with such patients was W. H. Rivers. He found the Freudian idea of dreams as 'wish fulfilment' unhelpful, instead suggesting that these dreams were attempts to *solve* a conflict. Another wrote:

The dream is simultaneously a reflection of the ways in which the mind is attempting to formulate the conflicts and problems of our lives and one of the means by which we attempt unconsciously to solve them.[5]

Building on this, recent theorists have argued that dreams reflect a level of thinking that is 'pre-logical'. A more common name for this might be 'intuition'. The dream becomes an arena for intuitive problem solving as well as for the evaluation and sorting through of the day's experiences.

By contrast, Wilhelm Stekel (1868–1940) concluded that Freud did not pay enough attention to dreams, and that they were so important that the dreamers could not be trusted to interpret their own dreams. Not surprisingly, Stekel saw himself as the one who could come to their aid! He was, in a sense, placing himself in the role of a seer or oracle — the one to whom others must come for the interpretation of their dreams.

The dreamer, he believed, could not be trusted, and would always attempt to conceal the real meaning of the dream. In this respect Stekel followed Freud's belief in the conscious mind's suppressing or censoring the dream. To get around this obstacle, he developed a vast catalogue of dream symbols. The symbols in a dream could be identified in the 'catalogue', and thus the correct interpretation found.

Such a reductionist approach, coupled with its denial of the dream, or the dreamer's, context, is clearly suspect. Unfortunately, 'formula dream interpretation', as this technique might be called, has immense popularity. There are plenty of books, magazine columns and radio talk-back hosts who are only too ready to tell people exactly what their dreams mean, speaking with a degree of certainty that is both irresponsible and unwarranted.

Descriptions of common symbols, as we will see later, can be useful, but they are simply guides, rather than sure-fire answers or a code to dream interpretation. Because dreams are primarily emotive, the feeling a symbol generates is as important as its content. Be wary of those who offer a guaranteed interpretation of your dream!

Carl Jung

Carl Jung (1885–1961) first met Freud in 1906. Within a few years, however, their initially close friendship was strained, and Jung was developing his own psychological theory. He founded a stream of psychotherapy he called 'analytical psychology', to differentiate it from Freud's psychoanalytic school.

Carl Jung did more than anyone else to develop a modern understanding of dreams and to translate the understanding of the human unconscious possessed by earlier societies into concepts that people in our society could understand. Jung (who was said to have examined more than 40 000 dreams from clients during his lifetime) was a deeply spiritual man who attempted to reconcile his objective observation of data from dreams with his belief that dreams represented our strivings for psychological health including, in particular, our need for spiritual growth.

Jung's particular strength, for our purpose, was the breadth of his knowledge: in relation to dream material, history, language, mythology, literature, religion, ethnology and many other areas. He was uniquely able to integrate material from his patients' dreams, and from the 'hallucinations' and 'delusions' of schizophrenics, with religious ideas (Eastern and Western), and the ideas of the gnostics, the alchemists, the I-Ching and many other sources. He had an unequalled ability to find the common threads and themes in human dreams, visions and other experiences of the unconscious in a great variety of situations and cultures.

Observing that there were similar symbols and motifs present in many cultures and traditions throughout history, Jung developed his theory of archetypes (explained in greater detail in chapter seven). These archetypes are innately present in the psyche of all people and are a fundamental part of the unconscious mind. Understanding and making use of the archetypes is a core element of Jung's approach to healthy psychological development.

Although built upon Freud's foundations, Jung's theories differed in many respects, several of which affected the way dreams might be understood and interpreted. In common with Freud, Jung saw the psyche being composed of an unconscious part and a conscious part. However, he also recognised an element he called the 'collective unconscious'. This contained the inherited material referred to above — symbols, abilities and archetypes — which were held in common with the whole of humanity, throughout history.

Rather than believing the conscious and unconscious dimensions to be in conflict, Jung thought that the unconscious sought to aid the growth of a person, providing a valuable and essential resource on the road to 'individuation' (or wholeness).

If the mind, then, was not in a permanent state of conflict, dreams became a helpful resource in this process, no longer concealing meaning, instincts or wishes, but rather *revealing meaning*.

Dreams were a part of normal health, not just a sign of neurosis. They served a purpose, and one should continually ask, 'What is the purpose of this dream?' which always pointed the dreamer forwards to growth and life.

Dreams were symbolic, not literal, and one needed to learn the language of one's unconscious. A vast number of symbols occurred within dreams, which were different dimensions of the psyche, and many that occurred in dreams were those that were neglected or considered inferior by the conscious self.

Unlike Freud, Jung had a cautious attitude towards any certainty in dream interpretation:

I have no theory about dreams; I do not know how dreams arise. I am altogether in doubt as to whether my way of handling dreams even deserves the name 'method'. I share all my readers' prejudices against dream interpretation as being the quintessence of uncertainty and arbitrariness. But, on the other hand, I know that if we meditate on a dream sufficiently long and thoroughly — if we take it about with us and turn it over and over — something almost always comes of it. This something is not of a kind that means we can boast of its scientific nature or rationalise it, but it is a practical and important hint which shows the patient [sic] in what direction the unconscious is heading him [sic].[6]

Dreaming was an involuntary process, not controlled by the conscious mind, and thus provided a wealth of material not normally consciously available. Using the idea of compensation, Jung saw that, in the dream, attention might be directed towards areas in the dreamer's life that had been overlooked or undervalued. Thus, the movement of the psyche was always towards balance and wholeness.

In working with dreams, it was emphasised that only the individual could correctly interpret his or her dream. It was a product of the dreamer's psyche, and its message was for his or her own growth. Its language, although symbolic, was best able to be understood by the dreamer, although others might assist in its revealing.

The dream had a religious purpose, too, in its drive towards wholeness, or what Jung called 'individuation'.

Reducing the dream to its individual components, and spending too much time and energy on any one image, might become counter-productive, as the overall theme, energy and purpose of the dream was what was important. For this reason, Jung tended not to use 'free association' in the way that Freud had. Seeking the overall theme meant that series of dreams were important, and it was more helpful to explore a collection of dreams rather than one in isolation.

Jung in many respects has come to be known as the father of modern dreamwork, due to his contribution to recovering dreams as a legitimate resource for those seeking wholeness.

Notes

1. Jung, C. G. 1966. *The Spirit in Man, Art and Literature*. Princeton, NJ: Princeton University Press. p. 85.
2. Freud, S. 1932. *The Interpretation of Dreams*. London: Norton.
3. Freud, S., ibid, p. 240.
4. Mattoon, M. 1978. *Understanding Dreams*. Dallas: Spring. p. 5.
5. Mackenzie, N. 1965. *Dreams and Dreaming*. London: Aldus. p. 236.
6. Jung, C. G. 1969. *Collected Works*, 16: 86. Princeton, NJ: Princeton University Press.

Psyche *(Courtesy Jeanette Tierney)*

6
A MODERN DREAMING

Psychology and Spirituality need to be seen as one ... Psychology is incomplete if it doesn't include spirituality and art in a fully integrative way.

Thomas Moore[1]

If we are interested in dreamwork and spirituality today, we are faced with a series of apparent dilemmas. If we look to the religious traditions in the West, we either encounter the suppression of a dreaming tradition or a very literalist 'visionary' approach. In the psychological arena, while dreams have come to be seen as a valuable tool by some schools, there is usually little attention paid to spiritual orientation.

Is it possible to bring the most positive aspects of each of these disciplines together in a creative and helpful way? The answer to this question must be 'yes', but we may have to shed some of our preconceptions along the way, whether we are travelling from a religious orientation or a psychological background.

Are Some Dreams of Divine Origin?

In the thirteenth century, Thomas Aquinas had suggested that there were two general classes of dreams — those divine in origin and those caused by the body. One of the problems that this distinction creates is how do you tell the difference?

Perhaps this is part of the appeal of a theory of dreams that is purely psychological. The problem of discernment is avoided, as all dreams have their origin within the psyche, even those that appear to be encounters with God. Any dream that seems to be prophetic in nature may be no more than a product of the unconscious mind.

Life would certainly be simpler if we could leave the matter there! However, for those who are seeking to develop a spiritual perspective, the Biblical attitudes, the Christian tradition and other religious traditions cannot be dismissed so conveniently. There is plenty of evidence, even among contemporary people, that sometimes a dream seems to have a significance, a power, an emotional dimension and direction well beyond the inner life of the dreamer.

It may be helpful to consider whether there are, in fact, two categories of dreams. First, there are 'encounter' dreams — relating to some sense of an experience of God. These are often described as seeming to originate outside of the dreamer's state, and appear quite clearly focussed, pointing the dreamer towards a particular course of action. Such dreams may be referred to as 'outer dreams'. Listening to the stories of people who have been called into ministry, for example, gives an insight into experiences of this sort.

Second, and far more common, are 'inner' or 'personal' dreams that are the product of our own psyche. These 'everyday' dreams are our primary focus, but before moving on to examine them in greater depth, it is important to examine briefly the nature of dreams that appear to be encounter experiences.

In defining these two broad types of dreams, we need to recognise that there is no clear distinction between the two. There may be times when a dream seems to have elements that are in common with both categories. A dream featuring a divine image, of, for example, Jesus Christ, Kali or Buddha, is not necessarily an 'outer' dream. The symbolic interpretation is what will be important. In another example, the appearance of a friend or acquaintance may seem to be inviting a very concrete response, of which no other meaning seems to be appropriate other than to respond with an action in waking life.

An appropriate question to ask at this point may be 'Does the dream carry a specific message, as opposed to simply revealing an issue, feeling or event?'

Divine, Numinous or Encounter Dreams

Many people seem to have dreams that they believe urge them to embark on a specific course of action and whose source of this urging is God. For this reason, some people have described these sorts of dreams as 'call dreams'. They are surprisingly common, and even people who would not describe themselves as religious may have had an experience where they have felt impelled to undertake a particular course of action presented in a dream.

In talking to people who believe they have had an encounter with God in a dream, certain things emerge. First, they often describe the experience as having an intensity beyond that experienced in their normal dreams. Second, the dream is generally treated as something that should be taken literally, rather than being purely symbolic. Third, the dream encourages the person to do something quite specific, such as making contact with someone or going to a particular event or place. For example, a woman dreamed that she was rung up by a friend she had not seen since her childhood, and that it was important for her to make contact. In a 'personal dream' the appearance of childhood figures is quite common, but in this specific case, the dreamer (who had embarked on dreamwork) felt compelled to respond to the dream literally because of the energy and focus it contained.

Marie-Louise von Franz, in her book *On Dreams and Death*[2], reminds us that sometimes in dreams, people encounter those who have died and that, if normal interpretation makes little sense, then one should consider taking the dream literally — as a real encounter with the dead person. She points out that questions about the reality of such encounters can only be answered hypothetically, but it pays to keep an open mind!

Prophetic Dreams

Dreams that appear to foretell an event hold a fascination all their own. From time to time, stories circulate about people who have had a dream containing a specific warning or where dreams seem to be an echo of a real event that occurs at a later time. Several dreams of this sort occur in the Bible (see chapters three and four).

Well-known historical examples include Bishop Lanyi and Abraham Lincoln. Lanyi dreamt of the death of Archduke Ferdinand in 1914. Unable to warn the archduke, he celebrated a mass for him on the morning of his death. Abraham Lincoln is said to have dreamt about his own assassination several days before he was killed.

On a more cautious note, however, we need to recognise that the mathematics of probability and the accuracy of recollection also come into play. In the latter, if a life event bears similarity to a dream event, we may unconsciously reconstruct the two to match. Probability comes into play when a relatively common dream event, for example, driving and crashing a car, is also a (relatively) common everyday experience. Mathematically, the chances of the two experiences coinciding for a few people are actually quite high!

There seems to be enough evidence to suggest that prophetic dreams do occur, but how and why they occur is a mystery. At the least they demonstrate the presence of a latent ability to transcend normal boundaries of time and space that we all share. As Jung put it in one of his last interviews:

> *You know, there are these peculiar faculties of the psyche that show it isn't confined to space or time. You can have dreams or visions of the future, you can see round corners and such things. Only ignorants deny these facts. It is quite evident that they do exist and have existed always.*[3]

The Difficulties of Discernment

The difficulties of discernment and interpretation of dreams that are believed to be prophetic or Divine should be apparent. We may have a sense that we are meant to 'do' something, but how do we decide if what we are being told is right or wrong, helpful or unhelpful?

The individual belief or revelation must always be examined within a broader community context, and compared to the ethical framework within which we operate, for example, the Christian tradition. If we wish to accept that dreams do occur that have a strong element of Divine revelation or immediacy, then we must be willing to subject them to the same scrutiny that we apply to 'revelations' and spiritual prompting in general. The Hebrew Scriptures in particular present a strong imperative for dreams, visions and, indeed, any form of revelation to be tested. As we have seen in previous chapters, dreams could be erroneous as well as helpful. Their source of error varied depending on the prevailing world view. They were simply misleading due to the type of dreamer or even because they acted as a 'test from the Lord' (Deut. 13), or they might originate from evil spirits or forces intent on mischief. The key principle though, remained the same. Did the dream event sit within the prevailing religious and social ethic or outside of it? A vision or dream that impelled a person to transgress these ethics, for example, by murder, would always be suspect.

For this reason, if we wish to work seriously with our dreams, no matter how we regard them and whatever purpose we perceive they have, it is advisable to find and work together with another, such as a spiritual director or therapist, who is able to assist in this process of discernment at all its levels. Some helpful guidelines for such work can be found in later chapters.

The Inner or Personal Dream

By far the most common sort of dream we have could be described as the 'personal' dream. Here we recognise that the energy, symbols and focus of the dream emanate from within ourselves. It is as if our unconscious uses dreams as one means to reveal to our conscious self some of the issues, thoughts and emotions that are affecting our lives, seeking to create awareness and to move us toward a resolution.

Within a framework of personal development, dreams also seem to perform certain functions. First, dreams offer us the inner resources of ourselves. Becoming aware of this material, and exploring it, is a means for personal growth and spiritual growth (see also below).

Second, dreamwork may function as a way for us to sort through the day's events, reflecting back to us our unconscious feelings about different incidents, people etc. and helping us to both ponder and memorise what has happened. Dreamwork may also give us opportunities to explore alternative options that we might have taken in a given situation. In this way, a person may learn from past experiences and be better equipped psychologically to deal with a future related issue.

An extension of this 'daily review' process gives rise to a third function. Here, a dream not only reviews life, but may point towards quite concrete solutions to life's problems. The unconscious part of our mind may offer a new way of tackling a question before us — a sort of unconscious lateral thinking. (We may have had this sort of experience, having a very clear course of action revealed, after going to sleep concerned and confused about something.) There are some very famous examples of dreams functioning in this manner. In the scientific arena, it is said that the chemist Kekule, while trying to understand the structure of benzene (in the days before organic chemistry), had a dream in which a number of snakes each seized the tail of another snake so as to form a circle: on waking, he was able to make an intuitive leap from the concept of a circle to the concept that benzene has a ring structure. Organic chemistry was born! In a similar fashion, Watson, working on the structure of DNA, is said to have dreamt of two intertwined snakes, after a period of frustrating struggle with the molecule's structure. And, in the field of literature, Robert Louis Stevenson ascribed important aspects of *The Strange Case of Dr Jekyll and Mr Hyde* as having their origins in a dream. Finally, the composer Tartini (1692–1770) credited one of his sonatas to music heard in a dream. For those interested in this area, these examples and many others are well described in Koestler's *The Act of Creation*.[4]

Integrating the Personal and the Divine

The recognition of two potentially different types of dreams, one being 'spiritual' and the other 'human-centred', does not necessarily lead to opposition. They can sit harmoniously together, linked by the simple concept that our unconscious, through dreaming, seeks to participate in and contribute to our waking self, and to encourage our total growth as human persons, made in the image of God, who live in relationship to one another.

To say that dreams primarily originate within ourselves does not then leave God, or spirituality, out of the picture. Our growth as human persons is of fundamental importance to God, and the God of incarnation is not distant from this activity. However, we may vary in our definitions of 'divinity'. Working with our inner self is an essential and inescapable part of spiritual awakening and growth.

A further point should be made, in that while we might talk of some dreams as being 'Divine revelation' and others as 'inner or personal dreams', the latter category, from a religious viewpoint, is no less revelatory. Rather, what is revealed is something about ourselves and our relationship with God and the world. In all our dreams, then, God as revealer, in the best sense of the word, can be seen to be at work.

Psychology and Spirituality

It is not surprising that many who seek a spiritual outlook on life have found Jungian psychology, with its emphasis on meaning and personal growth coupled with its interest in religious symbolism and universal nature, to be an environment where their religious framework can rest relatively comfortably, though not without challenge.

Details of Jung's approach will be outlined in chapters seven to twelve. For the present, we will say that Jungian psychology seems to offer a more positive, friendly and hope-filled face to the human condition, and is matched by the changing emphases in contemporary theology. Dreams become something to befriend, as part of befriending and loving ourselves, rather than something to flee, fear and suppress. The goal of the psyche, as movement towards health, wholeness and integration, is echoed in much theological and biblical imagery, and is linked with a strong sense of human responsibility. We are responsible for our own spiritual journey, our choices, actions, decisions and their consequences. When, on the other hand, the mind is in conflict, we are being controlled by forces within us that the ego can do little about. We become 'victims'. Of course, some people prefer to be victims, and some religious models like to create victims. If we are victims in this sense, we need not take responsibility for our lives. Religion that is victim-centred delights in taking control on its followers' behalf. Likewise, an approach to psychology that is conflict-based (like Freud's, for example) runs the danger of turning patients into victims, and taking over their lives and decisions instead of empowering them.

Some people from a more conservative religious background can have difficulty in accepting that psychology may have something to offer the person of faith. They have been brought up on a diet of hostility to and suspicion of the sciences. If we come to see that God is truly 'incarnational', this separation falls apart, for a healthy spirituality is able to perceive the movement of God in all things, including in contemplation and work on our own psyche. A creative dialogue and emerging synthesis of the rich insights both of the variety of spiritual traditions and the various models of psychology, opens up new possibilities for living. As Thomas Moore suggests, we will need to commit ourselves to this endeavour, from whichever discipline we work from, putting aside our prejudices and traditions in order to discover the 'sacred' and the 'soul' in everyday life.[5]

Spirituality, Community and Justice

Spiritual disciplines must link our inner life to the world around us. At first glance, dreamwork might seem to be diverting our attention from our responsibilities in the world. It is important to recognise that many forms of spirituality, and a fascination with the spiritual life, live in the shadow of such a danger. We can become so wrapped up with ourselves, and our own inner journey, that other people and events serve little purpose other than the manner in which they impact upon us. The act of giving something back to the world is lost.

One of the criticisms that can be levelled justifiably at the practice of some models of psychotherapy is that the focus can easily become egoistic, centring on enabling the individual to develop the power to make, live and enact life choices. At times, such a focus, if not held in balance, can develop into unhealthy self-centredness with the therapist consciously or unconsciously colluding with the client in the expression of this self-centredness under the auspices of being independent, assertive, looking after oneself, not carrying others' problems and so on. Such an approach becomes unhealthy when the context and web of relationships in which a person exists is not explored also. The goals of fulfilment and personal growth are not ends in themselves, but carry with them consequences and responsibilities that are to be expressed ethically in the outer world. Healthy personal growth does not negate but, rather, underpins these responsibilities.

Dreamwork shares in this tendency to self-preoccupation. But if we have a clear context in which our work is carried out, we will find ourselves constantly being drawn back into the world and invited to participate in its life rather than becoming disconnected from it. Laurence van der Post has said that one of the greatest contributions to the world and to peace individuals can make is the withdrawal of their projections.[6]

Projection is said to occur when we see our own inner material in an external person. In other words, we perceive the latter to have either the strengths we desire and are capable of but do not as yet own, or, quite often, our inadequacies and weaknesses. One of the most famous examples of (collective) projection in recent history is the way that the Nazis were able to induce negative projections by the German people onto the Jewish race. Recognising such projections, and then dealing with them, changes our way of relating to others — and almost always for the better.

Dreamwork can be a means by which we can identify some of our potential areas of projection. For example, a man might have a series of dreams over time that feature a beautiful woman who is his lover. If he were to know, or meet, someone who resembled this figure in real life, he might project his dream image onto the latter and fall in love with her. This is precisely what seems to happen to men, and women, in mid life. They discover and then fall in love with their contrasexual side — in the case of males, the undeveloped feminine side of their personality. Unrecognised as an element of themselves, it becomes transferred onto a woman, often one outside of their current relationship. Here we have the makings of the all too common mid-life affair. Very few of these relationships will last, as they are the creation of a projection, and are, in a sense, illusions. It is somewhat sobering when we realise we have begun to fall in love with an image of ourselves! If the projection can be recognised for what it is, then enormous personal growth is possible, and deeper and more mature relationships with both sexes may result. For a more detailed discussion of psychological approaches to the contrasexual side, the reader is recommended to chapter nine.

For couples approaching marriage, issues of projection and self-understanding can be critical. We all know the old cliche that 'opposites attract' is often true. We often seek in our partners the opposite attributes of our own ego personality. One of the things that can begin to happen, however, is that we relate to and through these persons through projections. We build a relationship, then, with partners as we imagine them to be, as our own psyche wants and needs them to be. When decide those people that they no longer wish to live as the constructed image, as they mature, problems result when one or both partners become dissatisfied with the other.

As we begin to withdraw the projections that we place on others, they are then truly able to be themselves, and a new level of intimacy in the relationship can result. If the projections remain, or if we fail to recognise them, along with the dependency cycles they create, then it is difficult for real growth in the relationship to take place. This process of withdrawal can be painful and threatening for both parties, so it is not surprising that often people prefer to continue to live with the illusions, or, when they begin to alter, abandon the relationship completely, and then start the whole process over again with another partner!

Learning about ourselves in this way, whether by dreams or other 'inner work', becomes the work of creating relationship and community. As a society, when men and women withdraw their projections of each other, and when we withdraw our projections from races, classes and cultures, a true sense of respect and community may develop. In this sense dreamwork, as part of balanced spirituality, becomes a justice-making activity. We will return to a specific example of the benefits of the withdrawal of projections at the end of the Dream Analysis Rules section of chapter fourteen.

As Jesus walked through the Palestinian countryside and shared the common life of the people he encountered, he left a legacy of changed and empowered people, who were encouraged to grow towards healing and wholeness, and to love and serve each other. This is the vision of the true direction and destiny of our spiritual journeying. Dreamwork, in its very best sense, can be an exciting resource for travelling this road. As Robert Ornstein says:

> *We do not usually consider the third of our life spent asleep as an opportunity for self-discovery. If we do return from our dreams with an image or a thought, it is personal, shared only once in a very great while with others. We have no psychological or cultural mechanism for allowing the dream consciousness to enrich the remainder of life.*[7]

It is to the task of beginning to understand and rediscover those basic tools that we now turn.

Notes

1. Moore, T. 1992. *Care of the Soul*. New York: HarperCollins. p. 15.
2. von Franz, M.-L.1989. *On Dreams and Death*. London: Shambala. pp. 15–16.
3. Jung, C. G. 1959. *Face to Face: Professor Jung*. Zurich: A & B Films.
4. Koestler, A. 1964. *The Act of Creation*. London: Hutchinson.
5. Moore, T. 1992. *Care of the Soul*. New York: HarperCollins. p. 15.
6. van der Post, L. 1977. *Remembering Jung*. Los Angeles: Bosustow Video Productions.
7. Jones, A. 1987. Would you like to hear my dream. In *British Journal of Religious Education*, Autumn. p. 31

Slow Mandala *by Jeanette Tierney*

7
THE LANGUAGE OF DREAMS

The soul is present with us as much while we are asleep as while we are awake; and while waking resembles active observation, sleep resembles the implicit though not exercised possession of knowledge.

Aristotle[1]

So far in this book, we have largely been concerned with the ways in which famous dreams, or types of dreams, have been interpreted in the past by great religious and psychological thinkers. For many of us, though, it is equally important, and often of more immediate value, to try to understand our own, everyday dream material, using whatever approach to interpretation seems to give most meaning. The questions that we tend to ask are: 'How can I, living an ordinary sort of life today, deal with my own dream material in such a way as to enhance my personal psychological and spiritual development?'; 'Why is it that I find my dreams so difficult to interpret?'; and 'Which of the myriad of ideas on the interpretation of dreams available today am I likely to find of greatest practical use?' The next sections of this book will attempt to address these questions.

When you first begin the attempt to understand your dreams, you will probably find it relatively easy to remember and record them (as described in chapter fourteen). That's the easy part. But, as soon as you try to interpret the imagery that you have collected, there will be a problem. You will have a mass of material that is emotionally powerful and seems to have meaning, but you won't be able to put that meaning into words or to give it a logical framework that you can relate to the rest of your life. This is just one example of the way that humans today are mystified by, and ignorant of, the workings of the unconscious mind.

One of the first things to strike anyone who makes a serious study of dream interpretation is how little we 'modern' humans know about the subject — far less, it would seem, than people living in biblical times and far less even than many tribal peoples living today. Thus, among the latter (for example, the Senoi of Malaysia), dream interpretation and dream sharing are a normal part of everyday life. Everyone shares, to a large extent, the same understanding of what the symbols found in dreams mean, and so a particular dream will have much the same meaning to every member of the group. They all have the same 'key' to dream meanings, in other words. We do not. Despite the claims of would-be populist experts, there is no simple and universally acceptable interpretation guide for our society.

There are at least two important reasons for this situation. First, and most obviously, we simply haven't been giving our dreams and visions the amount of time and attention we should. We spend almost all of the first twenty or thirty years of our lives (at least) concentrating instead on learning about, and adapting to, the external world and everything from history to traffic lights. This is necessary in our society today, of course. The information that we need to learn about the world is far more complex and changes much more rapidly than in tribal times. But we are still the same humans, with about the same learning capacity, so that the more we concentrate on the external worlds of mundane events the less time we have to look inside at our most important emotional and spiritual experiences.

You may find it helpful to use the analogy of how we learn to speak. We all learn to speak a primary language between the ages of one and five years, and with greater skill and in greater depth than we will ever speak a second language. If we, then, at a later age try to learn a second language, we will probably find this very difficult. We are most unlikely to be able to devote most of three or four years to the process. We will be constantly interrupted by the other priorities in our life, and will have forgotten much of the process of learning languages while we were doing other things. Very likely, too, our mind will be less flexible and able to learn than when we were young. So it is with dreams. By mid life most people will have spent a quarter of a century deliberately not understanding the symbolic language of the unconscious mind: a language they might have acquired very easily when they were young. Now they find themselves, often in middle age, trying to learn a 'second' language that is couched in symbols rather than words, and without textbooks or a universally known grammatical structure. It is a language that, when understood, provides information that very often challenges the assumptions on which their lives have been based. No wonder so many people give up the attempt as too difficult!

Second, and for at least the last 2000 years, humans have been moving more and more towards a position where aspects of ourselves that we regard as 'irrational' have either been disregarded or seen as dangerous or 'childish' (or both). Not just dreams and visions, but also all those techniques and approaches used in societies to help understanding of the inner world: from fairy tales and myths, through ritual and magic to inner religious experience. Fairy tales, for example, which are essentially parables of psychological development and its dangers and have been used to educate children and adults for thousands of years, were banished into the nursery only about two hundred years ago as fit only for children. They now seem likely to be banished entirely as too violent and instinctive (and politically incorrect) 'even' for children (see 'The Modern Fairy Tale').

Both modern Western science and organised Christianity must shoulder some of the blame for this situation. Ever since the Renaissance, Western science has tried to turn us away from a simple acceptance and celebration of creation (where the explicable and the inexplicable, or irrational, are both to be celebrated and accepted as part of God's gift), to a position where everything that cannot be reduced to its components and explained in objective terms should be viewed with suspicion and never simply accepted on its own terms. If dreams, for example, cannot be explained in terms of neural activity, or thought patterns, or sexual energy, they should never be used as guides to action, or taken to contain wisdom that the conscious mind cannot grasp! At least, not until science has come up with a 'proper' explanation!

Traditional, organised Christianity too, has often insisted that, out of the enormous range of human inner experiences, only a few represent 'true' Christian spiritual experience: the rest, all too often, being characterised as of demonic origin. And, more than this, both Christian and demonic experiences are 'put into' the individual by either God or the devil: they are not the possession of the experiencer. The effect of this sort of thinking has often been to deny the validity and importance of the individual's inner experiences. The latter are no longer considered to be important simply because that's how they feel to their possessor. They may be deceiving us; they may be of no importance, or evil and, in any case, they are not truly ours. As a result, the significance of a great majority of

The Modern Fairy Tale

Important manifestations of the human unconscious cannot ever be effectively banished from society. They simply reappear in other forms. Many of the themes from traditional fairy tales, for example, are to be found today in fantasy books and comics, films and computer games.

The film *The Silence of the Lambs* is one of many recent examples. Overtly a gruesome thriller about serial murders, it actually contains many of the psychological themes to be found in traditional fairy stories such as *The Beautiful Wassilissa*. In fairytale terms, the story follows the individuation path of a young female as she overcomes her father-complex: from the loss of the 'perfect', idealised father, through her encounter with a 'wicked' step-father (in turn, the rancher and the psychiatrist) and her journey into the unconscious (here a prison cell rather than the traditional forest) to bravely face the witch/ogre, to her achievement of personal liberation and recognition.

The story begins with the heroine running alone, sombre music and blue colour tones; it ends with her 'graduation' in a happy, social situation with warm colour tones. The early part of the film shows the heroine to be blocked and surrounded by masculine figures in every situation. Her liberation is symbolised by the killing of 'Buffalo Bill', a man who imprisons women in order to remove their skins and 'become' them (a wonderful image of a destructive masculine complex within a female psyche — a powerful, negative complex so often wants to overwhelm and replace ego-consciousness). The heroine is called out from her solitary journey to be given a task by the head of her training unit (who represents a real-life and non-neurotic father figure). She is given an impossible, and most unlikely, task — to interview the monstrous, cannibalistic Hannibal Lector (who symbolises the immensely powerful archetypal level, for both good and ill, of the great father). She is given careful instructions about the dangers of the task, which, in the very best fairy tale tradition, she immediately disregards. She becomes close to the 'monster'; she is utterly honest with him; she asks the right questions; she listens; she carries out the impossible tasks. Like

Wassilissa, like Gretel, she risks being eaten (overwhelmed) by an archetypal figure in order to achieve individuation. We learn that she has never overcome the death of the 'good' father, that her infant inner masculinity (symbolised by a lamb) was 'killed' by the 'wicked' rancher, that she is trying to stop this continuing death by living her good father's life (in the police), and that the lambs may stop crying if she can kill Buffalo Bill. Hannibal, in return, gives the heroine the gift of inner knowledge (as does Baba Yaga in *The Beautiful Wassilissa*): in this case, a lesson — almost a seminar — on the use of intuition. She uses her intuition to track down Buffalo Bill and release the imprisoned woman, together with the lamb-like little male dog. At the end of the film, the real-life father congratulates the heroine and says goodbye. Hannibal rings to say that he is going to dispose of the wicked step-father, as manifested in the psychiatrist (again, in the very best fairytale tradition). The heroine is left with her friends, including a potential, New Age Prince Charming (the boss-eyed zoologist): the next phase of individuation can now proceed.

The Silence of the Lambs has a relatively easily recognisable psychological content. But so also do countless other recent works, from *Star Wars* to *Brave Heart* (both actually variants of the myth of the hero). The next few chapters give guidelines for looking closely at films or other works that have particularly moved you. You may well gain self-knowledge from this process, just as in dream analysis.

important inner experiences is often disregarded or feared, rather than accepted as a part of the interweaving pattern that is the totality of the individual's inner reality.

Another important point that cannot be expressed too strongly is that most dreams and other inner experiences do not, and cannot fit into the traditional pattern of 'recommended' Christian experience. They are simply expressions of the totality of an individual's unconscious life. Much of the material will be related to everyday, mundane functioning, and some of the material that has a spiritual content may not fit easily into a Christian framework. Christianity, after all, is only one of many human paths to spiritual enlightenment: all of the great religions exist because they have been able, for many people and hundreds of years, to fulfil this human need. So it is scarcely surprising that the dreams and other inner experiences, even of committed Christians, seem to be nearer to Hindu, Jewish or other conceptions of the divine than to the Christian one (some examples of important 'pagan' dreams by Christian ministers will be described below). But this is nothing to be afraid of. It merely means that the dreamer has demonstrated the capacity for a variety of spiritual experiences. And it is a reflection of the great human ability to have spiritual experience and to create religious symbolism in any circumstances and at any time.

So, given our personal inexperience in the area, the indifference of most scientists to inner experience, and the controversial nature of the spiritual element of dreams, how can the individual learn to interpret his or her own dreams and visionary experiences in a way that has at least some objectivity, and which leads to spiritual and psychological growth? Let us begin by looking in some detail at the ideas of Carl Jung's direct and honest appraisal at the relationship between dreams and spiritual experience. Note that, as it can be difficult to explain some of his concepts without resorting to psychological language, a short glossary of the most important terms has been provided at the back of this book.

Jung's Theory of Archetypes

As noted above, it was Jung's observation that the same basic ideas and motifs have arisen (usually from the spontaneous experiences of individual humans) in all cultures, whatever the context of time or place, or of 'official' cultural thinking. These ideas and motifs find their way into myths, religious ideas, fairy tales, works of art and other expressions of the human psyche. One good example is the story of Cinderella (Aschenputtel), which, with three main variants, has appeared for over the last 2000 years in societies from India to Denmark and from China to Scotland. Another is the myth of the hero, of which the basic structure (the miraculous but humble birth, the early proof of extraordinary power, the tutor, the great deed done for the people, the appearance of hubris and the necessary death of the hero that consolidates the effects of his great deed) has appeared in every known society — to our knowledge — from Gilgamesh through Nu-Jeki Spasu (of the Quebec Mickmack Indians) and the Welsh hero Pwll, to Samson, Orpheus and Siegfried.

Jung's belief was that these themes, ideas and motifs represent basic human mental structures and/or abilities, perhaps related to universally experienced situations. They represent the fundamental structures of our unconscious minds. They are always alive in us (whether or not we have ever used them, or encountered the situation to which they relate), and they are innate (inborn). To Jung, it wasn't possible (or important) to decide whether they were the products purely of evolution or an original part of creation (and therefore the pattern of God within us). In either case, they include all our potential for religious experience.

Jung called these themes 'archetypes' (literally 'implanted from the beginning') and saw them as forming a meshwork of abilities, from the very simple to the very complex and important. He believed that psychological health was a matter of understanding and using our archetypal abilities as much as possible — that this would lead to dynamic mental harmony and a religious approach to life. And that, if the archetypes were unrecognised, unused or suppressed by consciousness, they would simply live on in our unconscious— and torment us in our dreams! He also emphasised, very strongly, that the most important archetypes are unconscious motifs of enormous power, compared to which ego consciousness seems very small and unimportant. So that, when the ego ventures into the unconsciousness during dreaming, it can be overwhelmed by the emotional and numinous power of archetypal imagery. We will discuss the nature of the archetype of the self in chapter twelve, and its relationship to the God-image, but for now it is sufficient to understand that the usual (and correct) attitude of ego-consciousness, when presented with powerful archetypal imagery, is one of humility and perhaps worship.

At this point, it is perhaps appropriate to look at a couple of the hazards and difficulties of analysing one's own dreams.

First, when a dream contains powerful archetypal contents, it is very difficult for the dreamer to make an objective interpretation. Even when to any outside observer the meaning of the dream seems very obvious, the dreamer will be caught up in the emotions within the dream and may not be able to see the overall meaning from an observer's perspective. An example of this is a young man who had the following dream:

The whole world was a gold mine, within which all the men were employed as miners. Unfortunately, however, there was a male monster living within the mine shafts. It was a huge, fierce, ugly, old monster and it was gradually killing and eating all the miners. There was no hope.

The dreamer was unable to interpret the dream, or to produce associations to it (feelings, thoughts, events or memories that are aroused when the imagery of the dream is contemplated). So he was asked to draw the monster. The drawing was remarkable and very different indeed to the verbal description of the dream. The world was shown as small, barren and rocky. On the surface stood a little baby monster with tears running down his face. He was watching a spaceship taking off, in which was a grinning mummy-monster. The drawing was very powerful, but there was no aggression, just sadness and loneliness.

At this point, it was suggested to the dreamer that perhaps the monster was not so big, old and destructive as he seemed. Perhaps he represented the anger of a child who felt abandoned, perhaps by a mother figure. The reaction was a violent denial. No! The monster was old, male and ferocious. It lived under the ground — it was never on the surface — and it would never stop until it had killed every human on the planet! This is a strong example, but it is not unusual. The dreamer was caught up in his fear of the monster (very likely his own infantile rage, itself a reaction to feeling abandoned) and could not acknowledge with his conscious mind something that some other part of him knew well enough to draw.

> *... man is an enigma to himself. This is understandable, seeing that he lacks the means of comparison necessary for self-knowledge ... as a conscious, reflecting being, gifted with speech, he lacks all criteria for self-judgment.*[2]

This general rule, that it is usually easier to interpret another person's dream than your own, is Dream Analysis Rule One in chapter fourteen. This chapter examines the most important general rules for dream analysis in more detail than is possible in the general text. Further references will be made to it in the next few chapters.

A second hazard of analysing one's own dreams is simply the danger of being overwhelmed by archetypal unconscious contents (see also Dream Analysis Rule Two in chapter fourteen). If these are very powerful and negative, and ego-control is weak, it is sometimes better not to look at dream material, but to do so only slowly and with the help of a therapist, because of the danger of bringing up material (hitherto repressed) that the dreamer's consciousness is unable to control. You can go off your head, in other words. This, really, is a danger that we should all bear in mind. Madness is actually freely available to all of us in the right circumstances:

no one has an ego so strong that it cannot be overwhelmed. Edward Edinger, a well-known American Jungian, has described this danger in a number of books and tapes (see also the further reading list at the back of this book). He is particularly concerned with the dangers inherent in looking too closely and too long at the central archetypal image of the self, the connection to the God-image. Several times he cites Friedrich Nietzsche as an example of a modern man who, in attempting to look at and understand this image from a modern (psychological) viewpoint, became overwhelmed and lapsed into madness. His conclusion is that Nietzsche fell because he neglected to read the warnings and rules for such investigations in the Bible (and other religious books). Edinger makes the interesting point that Jung was very aware of the reasons for Nietzsche's collapse, and took care to limit his own encounters with archetypal material as a result.

Let us now return to the concept of the archetypes. If we look at the most important of these — the shadow, the persona, the animus or anima, the child, the guide, the great mother, the trickster, the hero, the night journey and the self — we will be able to do two things at once. We will be able to see what Jung thought of as the normal process of healthy human psychological development (which he called individuation) and to work out specific meanings and ways of interpreting at least some dreams that contain important archetypal material.

Notes

[1] Parrinder, G. (ed.) 1990. *Collins Dictionary of Religious and Spiritual Quotations*. Glasgow: HarperCollins. p. 83
[2] Jung, C. G. 1957. *The Undiscovered Self*. New York: Penguin (Mentor). pp. 55–6.

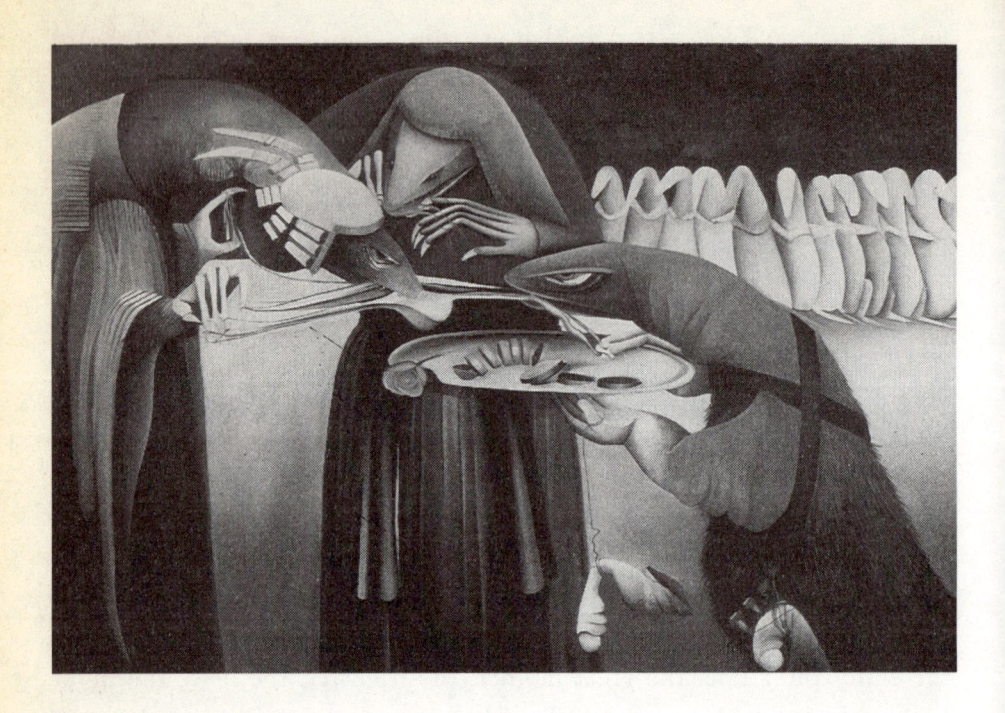

Feeding Time — *images from a dream by Nina Anisimova*

8
THE SHADOW

True, whoever looks in the mirror of the water will see first of all his own face. Whoever goes to himself risks a confrontation with himself. The mirror does not flatter, it faithfully shows whatever looks into it...This confrontation is the first test of courage on the inner way, a test sufficient to frighten off most people, for the meeting with ourselves belongs to the more unpleasant things that can be avoided so long as we can project everything negative into the environment. But if we are able to see our own shadow and can bear knowing about it, then a small part of the problem has already been solved.

Carl Jung[1]

The shadow was conceived by Jung as being one of the most important of the archetypes. It is often described as an 'alter ego' — the person we might have been but are not — containing many of our most important emotions and instincts, some at least of our potential for evil, and many repressed memories.

The shadow is something that everyone (in our society) creates as they grow up. We are all born multipotential with the capacity to survive and develop in a variety of ways, after all. We have to be because of the enormous variety of circumstances in which people live. One might be born as Prince Charles, a Somali peasant or a Bosnian Muslim — it is all a matter of luck really. This being so, we all need an enormous range of adaptive abilities, so that we can survive — and, hopefully, prosper — in almost any circumstance. And this is not just a matter of physical survival capacity: it is a matter of psychological adaptability, too. Our life might require us to be introverted or extroverted, emotionally expressive or controlled, spiritual or earth-bound, loving or cold. But requirements will be made. We will have to make more use of some parts of our potential and neglect others.

So the average child is born, full of potential, into a particular life situation. He or she will, as time goes on, learn more and more to become a particular ego personality. It will be a matter of chance and choice: of chance because of the specific demands of the environment (for example, living in a family where relationships are governed by interpersonal warmth) and of choice because, little by little, the child will find that it has a natural affinity for some personality attributes rather than others, or that certain ways of being 'work' for it. (Take, for example, the naturally cool-natured child who finds that it is rewarded for developing its capacity for warmth more than it might do otherwise.) All of this, slowly and surely, develops the characteristic and complicated ego personality that we 'are'.

But, as we develop our ego personality, we also do something else at the same time. What has happened to all those parts of our original potential that we didn't develop? They won't just cease to exist: they will still be there, as potential or as partly developed, then rejected, personality attributes, and they will live on in the unconscious as an alternative to the waking ego. So, by the very act of creating a specifically delineated ego-personality, we have also created its opposite in the unconscious. This is the shadow. Everyone has one. It is the person we could have been but are not — either through choice or lack of opportunity. Note here, though, that the shadow may be an individual one (as described above) or collective. All human groups, large or small, will have a collective distillation of their individual shadows, a universally recognised group alter ego. Where the individual shadow is most often manifested in the individual's dreams or life, the collective shadow will be manifested in group attitudes, for example, the attitude of one nation to another, or in 'great' works of art that strike a chord for millions of people within a group or nation over a long period of time.

The nature of the shadow is very well understood in many tribal societies. It is frequently seen as the 'inner friend' who sits on your shoulder, gives you advice and accompanies you all your life. Often it is seen as an animal, with particular properties: usually properties that provide a necessary balance to the ego personality and that connect the latter to instinctive or spiritual wisdom. The shadow is also described in all those hero myths where the hero is accompanied by a 'friend', a near-equal who is often seen as primitive and instinctual, but possessing magical or physical abilities that the hero lacks: Enkidu to Gilgamesh, for example, Lancelot to King Arthur, or Han Solo and Wookie to Luke Skywalker in *Star Wars*. There seems to be no particular 'problem' about this sort of shadow figure. It is generally seen as both benign and essential to normal psychological functioning. It has properties that the ego lacks but needs to have available in emergencies. It is often primitive and sometimes brutal, true, but it is essentially the ego's friend.

In modern Western society, though, the shadow is problematical for us, for several reasons, first, and most obviously, because it is so unfamiliar to us. Characteristically, in the dreams of a modern human, the shadow will appear as something (or someone) strange and exotic. Second, because we value consciousness and 'objective' logic so much, much of our instinctive, emotional and 'animal' nature has become unfamiliar to us and resides in the shadow. Third, and perhaps especially in Christian societies, much of our instinctive sexuality and aggressiveness is often rejected as evil and unchristian, perhaps even as demonic. If we have a dream of an exotic species of animal that radiates demonic energy and an aggressive sexuality, we may be seeing no more than an aspect of our own shadow — an aspect that we don't know, that we fear, that we despise, and that we are no longer able to access via conscious inner work or communally shared myth or ritual.

A word of warning at this point, though. Whether or not one believes in a personal devil, it is important to know that the shadow does contain some aspects of our unconscious life that are truly evil. We all have, for example, the ability for psychopathic disregard and aggression towards others. This ability is a counterbalance to, and is created by our development of, the ability to care for others and behave altruistically. It can also be argued that we have to have psychopathic abilities as well as caring ones. Hopefully, the average human will never need to use them in her or his lifetime, but there are rare occasions when necessity might demand their use. In any case, and whether we ever need to use them or not, these negative abilities belong in the shadow. One therefore has to be as careful as possible, when dealing with the shadow and trying to understand those aspects of it that we need to understand, or hope to use, not to also bring up and let loose (or, even, be overwhelmed by) the elements of evil that share the same house.

At an everyday level, though, shadow elements are some of the most frequently seen dream images. They are usually manifested as human beings of the same sex as the dreamer. They will usually have a strong, emotional effect on the ego — often a negative one. Many Jungians have stated that the first encounter with their shadow in dream analysis is almost always a negative one. We may encounter an unknown person who seems very aggressive or radiates some other unacceptable property. Sometimes the shadow figure will resemble someone we actually know in waking life but who, for us, is the epitome of some particularly unpleasant personality characteristic, be it dishonesty, amorality, stupidity or whatever. In either case, we will be looking at some unacceptable (shadow) aspect of ourselves; our own aggressiveness, or amorality or selfishness, for example. Its nature will depend precisely on what it is about ourselves that we most despise, reject or fear. What should we do about it?

First of all, we don't *have* to do anything about it! Encounters with unpleasant shadow elements in a dream merely signify an honest self-observation. However, if we wish to do so, we can choose to set about understanding them and perhaps bringing them up towards consciousness and incorporating their positive properties into our waking life. Some practical guidelines as to how to proceed with this are given in chapter fourteen, and some references for further reading can be found in chapter sixteen. For the present, let us just look at a couple more general rules.

First (Dream Analysis Rule Three in chapter fourteen), when a dream motif is recurrent and particularly powerful (if, for example, it wakes us up several times), this is a strong indication that analysis may be in order. At the very least a powerful shadow motif suggests that a lot of unconscious energy is being invested into an unconscious compensation for a one-sided waking attitude. Another sign that a dream motif has a lot of unconscious energy and should perhaps be attended to, is when it appears as multiple figures: if we are attacked by a lion in a dream, for example, that's bad enough, but three lions attacking us would be absolutely demanding that we take notice!

Second (Dream Analysis Rule Five in chapter fourteen), we should try as hard as possible not to be emotionally overwhelmed by what the dream *seems* to say about shadow elements. We have already discussed this dimension in connection with the dream of the gold mine world and its 'monster' in the previous chapter. When we meet shadow images, they will often seem very aggressive, for example. But are they? Check it out. Look at the dream again to see if the shadow images actually did (or even said) anything that was truly aggressive. One of the commonest findings in dream analysis is that a dream in which a shadow element is seen to be hostile is actually characterised by hostile actions towards the shadow on the part of the ego. The dreamer might say, for example, 'I dreamed I was walking in the woods and I met a huge big aggressive bear: it was going to kill me ... how do I know? Well, I felt it was going to ... no it didn't actually do or say anything. I didn't let it. I killed it before it could hurt me!' That sort of thing.

Finally, although we have written above as though shadow elements always appear in dreams as human figures, this is very often not the case.

They may also be represented as animals or even plants or objects. It is often suggested by Jungians that human dream figures represent elements of the psyche that are at the level of, or can be brought to, conscious understanding, whereas animal and other dream figures represent elements of the psyche that are 'below' the level of consciousness and perhaps more instinctive. And, as Marie-Louise von Franz has stated in a number of her books on the subject of fairy tales, shadow elements that appear as animals in dreams often transform later on into human figures as they become assimilated with, or recognised by, consciousness. At the very least, after experiencing a non-human shadow figure, say, a dog, one should ask oneself why the conscious mind thinks of this particular element of psychological energy as being 'dog-like'. Does this suggest stupidity, perhaps, or instinctiveness, or faithfulness? What is dogginess to *you*?

Notes

[1] Jung, C. G. 1969. *Collected Works*, 9i: 43–4. Princeton, NJ: Princeton University Press.

Anima *(Photo by David Haynes)*

9
ANIMUS AND ANIMA

Difficult and subtle ethical problems are not invariably brought up by the appearance of the shadow itself. Often another 'inner figure' emerges. If the dreamer is a man, he will discover a female personification of his unconscious; and it will be a male figure in the case of a woman. Often this second symbolic figure turns up behind the shadow, bringing up new and different problems. Jung called its male and female forms 'animus' and 'anima'.

Marie-Louise von Franz[1]

'Animus' and 'anima' are Jung's terms for the contrasexual part of the psyche. The animus is the masculine aspect of a woman's psyche, the anima the feminine aspect of a man's psyche. Jung considered that everyone has such a contrasexual side and that it is of the utmost importance (he sometimes said that it represented forty-nine per cent of our genetic makeup). Its development, like that of the shadow, is an inevitable accompaniment to ego development. Thus, as we grow up and develop specific, conscious ego characteristics, other parts of the psyche that the ego cannot (or will not) develop, because they represent the psychological characteristics of the opposite sex, are likely to become a part of the animus or anima.

As we might expect, the individual anima or animus will be very much a reflection of the society in which the individual lives and of the individual's personal experiences as to what constitutes the opposite sex. As a result, the anima/animus figures that Australians see today in their dreams are often very different to those described by Jung half a century ago. It is very much a matter of debate whether the animus and anima are no more than one's personal concept of the opposite sex or whether they have certain universal characteristics in all humans — whether, in fact, they are representatives of universal masculine and feminine principles within everyone. For those interested in this issue, we would recommend the writing of Robert Johnson (particularly *The Psychology of Romantic Love*) and Emma Jung's *Animus and Anima* (see also the reading list in chapter sixteen). For the purposes of the present book, we will usually discuss the animus and anima in relation to the individual's personal understanding of the opposite sex.

The anima or animus is normally seen in dreams as a person, or animal, of the opposite sex. In life, it will be characteristically projected upon a member of the opposite sex — a process that is, of course, the basis of falling in love. When we fall in love, we see in another person everything that is beautiful, divine and erotic about our own contrasexual side. The projection has all the numinous power of unconscious material, so that we feel overwhelmed by its presence — and often inferior to it. Often, we feel the need to worship it. Later on, when the projection is withdrawn (as inevitably happens after a while) and we can clearly see the person that we were in love with, we may discover (as Jung said on several occasions) that we 'have made a hell of a mistake'.

In dreams, as in life, visions of the anima or animus can be overwhelming, and fill us with a sense of love, eroticism and/or worship. We may see an unknown man or woman of incredible beauty or seductiveness or our best friend's spouse — at which point it is a good idea to bear a few principles in mind.

First, everything that we see in a dream is a part of our own psyche (see also Dream Analysis Rule Five in chapter fourteen). All the beauty, emotion and strength that we perceive in a dream, or project onto someone else, is our own — a part of our unconscious nature. This knowledge can give us an understanding of our own inner beauty and strength, and without inflation because, very clearly, the properties that we see are not possessed by the 'front mind' — they do not belong to the ego, but are the possessions of or gifts from the unconscious.

Second, and following from the above, the things that we see in a dream are not really other people. So, if we see our best friend's husband or wife in a dream, fall in love with them and make love to them, it doesn't mean that we have actually or morally committed adultery. And it certainly doesn't mean that we should then act out the dream in real life! We would very quickly find out what a mistake we were making. What has happened is that we have seen our contrasexual side and that, for reasons of its own, our unconscious has decided to give it our best friend's spouse's face. It is likely that, in some way, there is a resemblance between our inner contrasexual side and the person in the dream: a degree of 'match' that allows the projection to occur. But the resemblance can be very slight — an attitude in common, a feeling, tone in a particular situation and so on. Our 'dream mechanism' is really just putting the nearest, matching face onto an internal mental structure. So the rule here is always to be careful to differentiate between our objective knowledge of real people in everyday life and internal dream objects that superficially resemble them (see also Dream Analysis Rule Nine in chapter fourteen).

When, therefore, we have a powerful, erotic animus/anima dream, and are disturbed by the resemblance between the dream image and someone that we know in real life, with whom an erotic relationship would not be right, it is often helpful to spend a little time making an objective comparison of the two figures. We will find, almost inevitably, that the dream figure possesses properties that the real-life figure does not. It will be more beautiful, or stronger, or more numinous, or younger, perhaps. The differences between the two figures can then be seen, without any possibility of dispute, as purely our own unconscious material — pure anima/animus, if you like. Once we have been able to see that a part of the dream figure is the creation of our own mind, the spell is often broken and it becomes much easier to see the entire dream image as separate from the real-life person.

Actually, the same rule applies to the projected properties that we (incorrectly) see in the loved one when we fall in love. Depending on circumstances, this may be a most useful way of avoiding trouble or spoiling the fun of being in love. After all, if we are in love with someone, the projections will eventually come off of their own accord. We will have to decide for ourselves whether seeing the eternal feminine or masculine in our partner is a good or bad thing.

Third, a healthy relationship between the ego and the anima/animus should be a close one, and often a relationship with strong erotic overtones. The anima or animus is often described as one's 'soul-mate' — the other half that makes the psyche complete. Case studies and world literature are full of examples of people for whom the anima/animus represented creative or spiritual fulfilment. This being so, and given that the anima/animus has the properties of the opposite sex, one of the commonest images of anima/animus dreams is of sexual union: often of a beautifully erotic nature. This isn't always the case, of course. Other common images of such dreams include working together, talking together in a very intimate way, or even a physical union where the two bodies (ego and anima/animus) fuse together in a non-sexual way. But, at least in our society, sexual imagery tends to be the most common and the most powerful. Dreams in which one has sex with the animus or anima should, therefore, be taken as an eroticised image of closeness or union with the contrasexual side, and therefore as a very positive event. They are neither literally nor morally the same as having real-life sex with the person that the anima/animus appears to resemble (see also Dream Interpretation Rule Eight in chapter fourteen). Of course, if one is sexually frustrated, anima/animus dreams are more likely to be sexualised. This is a confounding variable that should not distract us from the positive nature of union with our contrasexual side. After all, so far as the unconscious is concerned, if a dream can serve the double function of sexual release and an encounter with the anima/animus, so much the better!

On a more serious note, the way in which the animus or anima appears in a dream can tell a great deal about the ego-animus/ego-anima relationship. We have already seen how the figure may have great beauty and erotic or spiritual energy. The relationship of anima/animus to creativity is also well documented. Perhaps the most famous example is that of Dante and Beatrice. Beatrice was a young girl whom Dante, the great pre-Renaissance writer, glimpsed, for a moment, only once. Yet the brief vision was such that she became the inspiration of his greatest writings. Many other writers and artists have talked about an inner 'muse' whose presence is necessary for their creative work. So if we have a dream in which we enter a new relationship, or go on a journey with a numinous anima/animus figure, we should look for evidence in our life of, or at least potential of, new abilities or opportunities for creative work in the broadest sense. A characteristic example of this sort of role for the anima/animus is given in Emma Jung's description of a dream experienced by an over-rational 'desiccated' young man, as follows:

I was going through a dense wood; then, there comes toward me a woman enveloped in a dark veil, who takes me by the hand and says that she will lead me to the wellspring of life.[2]

Another, more recent example, illustrates the same principles. In the helping professions, a 33-year-old man was contemplating leaving one job in a regional town and returning to the city, but was in a state of uncertainty about his abilities in taking another position, due to many difficulties and disappointments in his current role:

I am walking along a beach, and there is a beautiful red sailing boat pulled up on shore. Next to the boat is a beautiful woman [who he was convinced was Aphrodite]. I am instantly in love with her, and drawn to her. She smiles at me, and with enormous compassion, says, 'If you return to the city, I will teach you to sail'.

The dream showed the man that, through his feminine side, he would learn and be able not only to survive, but 'sail' on the waters of the unconscious, and gain renewed creativity and abilities necessary for his vocation. He is also confronted with the beauty of his feminine side. It is also interesting to note the powerful emotional attachment to the anima figure. After working with the dream, he discovered the strength to make the move to the city, continue with his profession in a new way and write a series of published books. The man also commented that he was well aware that if he met someone in waking life that resembled her, he would fall hopelessly in love with her.

Additionally, it is worth noting that animus and anima figures are often related to spirituality and religious energy. In our culture, creative energy, which seems to be closely related to a sense of spirituality (as in the quotations above), is nearly always identified with the anima/animus. Very often, the anima or animus will act as a guide for spiritual and creative renewal. It is not surprising, then, to discover how often they appear in dream material. The role of the anima and animus as creative archetypes, though, can be considered to be a strong statement about the lack of creativity in the everyday lives of people in our culture. Both men and women, for hundreds of years, have seen creativity as residing in a mysterious, contrasexual figure that lives in the unconscious and hardly ever as an everyday part of our conscious lives.

So far, we have talked about the animus or anima as a positive figure. But many people see the animus/anima, just as they do the shadow, as hostile and/or indifferent, particularly on first meeting — perhaps as an aggressive chauvinist, or a feminist with a castrating knife. As is the case with the shadow, this tells us something about the individual's psychological development. First, and most obviously, that ego-consciousness has the attitude that this part of the unconscious is hostile, or does not love it as it should. This may, in fact, mean that it is the ego that is hostile or unloving (as discussed above in connection with the shadow), often because it does not know or understand the anima/animus, and projects its own anger or fear onto it. Or it may mean that the anima/animus is 'angry' with the ego, in which case one needs to know why. Some dreams dealing with this issue are detailed in chapter thirteen. For the moment, it is important to remember that the fundamental nature, or instinct, of the animus/anima is to act as a loving and intimate counterpart of the ego: a friend or an inspiration, not an enemy. To Jung, dynamic harmony between the archetypes is the instinctive and normal state of the psyche, while great hostility and tension between them always represents an artificially created abnormal state. If hostility is really present, it is absolutely vital to know why. What is the ego doing, or what has happened in the life of that person, to create hostility where none should exist? To answer this question, the ego has to hold a dialogue with the hostile anima/animus figure (as described in chapter fourteen) and discover what the latter needs in order to remedy the situation. As we will see later, the most usual need is simply to be recognised and utilised.

Another finding, which can be quite startling to the dreamer, is to find that many forms of the animus and anima don't play traditional sex roles. Presumably they did until about the 1960s, until which time we all 'knew' that men were tough, logical and emotionless, while women were soft, fluffy things that operated on a feeling basis. The literature about the dreams of men and women most certainly, until the last couple of decades, gave these attributes to the animus and anima respectively: the animus, in dreams, then represented the tough, cool male side of the 'traditional' woman; the anima the soft, feminine underbelly of the 'real man'. It's not so any more! Anyone who practices Jungian dream analysis in Australia today rapidly becomes familiar with women with cool, thinking ego-personalities, who have a warm, cuddly (but still clearly male) animus, and relationship-oriented feeling men whose animas are cool, tough and logical. This is very much as it should be. The abilities for cool logic and warm relatedness, for ruthlessness and for emotionality, are present in all of us and one can't, nowadays, predict in which direction the development of the ego personality may go in either a man or a woman. This being so, the animus/anima (and often the shadow too) will tend to adopt the opposite characteristics, as part of a healthy compensation for the waking ego attitude.

Finally, there is often a fine line to be drawn between dreams or visions of the anima/animus and of parental images. The great father and great mother will be discussed briefly in the next section. For the present, we would like to make the obvious but often overlooked point that, when we are young, the first images of the opposite sex that we acquire from life are likely to be those of the parent of the opposite sex. In a developing male, for example, the guiding inner woman starts off as his mother. Freud understood this very well when he described the Oedipus complex (in a girl, the Electra complex). In a man with an Oedipus complex, the inner image of the feminine has got stuck at the mother-image stage and cannot change. In healthy development, the inner contrasexual image gradually changes, as more people of the opposite sex are experienced, and perhaps also as the innate, individual archetypal animus/anima develops as part of an instinctive process of maturation. If this development doesn't occur, the inner contrasexual image remains, or is still dominated by the mother or father. In this case, the ego is all too likely to remain at a childish level when encountering such images, instead of dealing with them in a mature way as their equal.

In summary, the animus and anima are the archetypal, unconscious contrasexual elements that are present in all of us. They represent personal experiences of the opposite sex. They are usually seen in dreams or visions as people or animals of the opposite sex, often people that we know, but don't (and shouldn't) have an intimate relationship with. In life, they may be projected upon members of the opposite sex, with whom we may then fall in love. Dreams of the animus/anima may be overwhelming or upsetting because they may suggest erotic relationships with forbidden others: it is important to remember that the 'people' we see in dreams are actually parts of ourselves and not the same as the real-life people they resemble. The ego-animus/ego-anima relationship is naturally a close one, often visualised in erotic terms: the animus/anima may also act as a guide or inspiration towards creativity or union with one's contrasexual abilities. When the animus/anima is hostile, this always means that there has been a disruption to the ego-animus/ego-anima relationship during development. Often the latter will be found to have been neglected or repressed. The anima/animus may not resemble traditional views of the masculine or feminine, rather, it will have characteristics that compensate for, or balance, those of the conscious ego. Finally, the animus and anima have their roots in childhood parental images. With maturation, these rather overwhelming images become replaced by those of the companion, lover or inspiration.

Notes

[1]. von Franz, M.-L. 1964. The process of individuation. In C. G. Jung and M.-L. von Franz (eds), *Man and His Symbols*. London: Aldus. p. 177
[2]. Jung, E. 1957. *Animus and Anima*. Dallas: Spring. p. 67.

Great Father Archetype

10
THE GREAT MOTHER, THE GREAT FATHER

God's gift, sent from above,
a real unselfish love
I found in my mother's eyes.

Traditional English song

The great mother and the great father are archetypal parental images that are inborn in all of us. We will deal principally with the great mother here, as far more has been written about her than her male counterpart. This, incidentally, tells us something about the upbringing of Jung and the other male psychologists who have contributed most in this area, and, also, in a more general way, about the relative importance of the mother in our society in the upbringing of both male and female children.

The Great Father Archetype

Much of what has been said regarding the great mother can also be applied to the archetype of the great father. A maturation process of healthy separation is equally important. For girls, the father archetype, at its best, provides a pathway for developing affirming secure relationships with males, and a sense of their own masculine energy.

For boys, the father archetype is absolutely critical to their healthy development, teaching them about appropriate expressions of strength, competition and emerging self-assurance and progress into manhood. Without adequate 'father imagery', or with unhelpful imagery, many child–parent issues will remain unresolved, and are often carried into other relationships.

In Western society, though, there are other factors that seem to affect the functioning of this archetypal ability. Since the Industrial Revolution, the role of 'father as parent' can be described more by absence than presence. Moved into a structured work environment, away from the family for most of the day, male involvement in child-rearing has changed dramatically, with negative consequences for both girls and boys. Perhaps this absence contributes to the relative scarcity of references to this archetype in the literature, particularly before the last two decades.

The role of the great father can clearly be seen in fairy tales, ancient and modern. *Silence of the Lambs* contains the essence of this (see chapter seven); Robert Johnson's *He* spells out the Parsifal myth as a path for male individuation[1], and Robert Bly explores the tale of Iron John, especially in relation to the absent father[2]. Further ideas are developed in the works of Andrew Samuel[3]. Readers who are interested in this area would also do well to read the Australian author Steve Biddulph's book *Manhood*[4].

A second complication arises because religious traditions have ascribed, directly or indirectly, male gender imagery to concepts of God, invariably with a consequent loss of feminine imagery. As we are discovering, god-images in dreams need to be approached with caution, many questions needing to be asked to discover their essence and meaning.

The Great Mother Archetype

The archetype of the great mother is an inborn capacity in all humans to recognise, and respond to, anyone and anything that is able to symbolise some part of everything that the human mother can be (or, better, might seem to be). An understanding of the archetypal great mother begins with the acceptance that we have no guarantees about the sort of person our real-life mother is. She may be a self-sacrificing, all-loving mother, or a cold, unloving and selfish reluctant parent. She may be warm and cuddly or aggressive, spiritual or brutal, consistent or ever-changing. Every baby would prefer to have a warm, loving and devoted mother, of course, but she or he will have to adapt to the nature of the real mother in the end, by forming a bond with the real mother, in order to survive.

Now, we have already seen above that we are all born multipotential in terms of ego personality, and that this 'overkill' in terms of potential leads to the creation of the archetype of the shadow. In a similar way, we are all born with a multipotential inner image of the great mother. This must encompass every possibility: everything that mothers ever have been or could be — both positive and negative. The possession of an archetype of this sort means that, whatever our real-life mother is actually like, she will

Great Mother Archetype

correspond to at least one of the aspects of our inner 'great mother'. We will, then, be able to 'recognise' her as 'mother' and project the whole of the positive aspect of the archetypal great mother image on to her. We will love and worship her, at least for a few years, as the living, outward personification of the inner archetype.

As you can imagine, the great mother is seen in dreams via an enormous range of symbolic images. On the positive side she may be represented by anything that is supportive, nourishing, loving and protective: a cow, perhaps, a fairy godmother, the Virgin Mary, a warm, womb-shaped cave, or even a bowl of fruit! On the negative side she may appear as the wicked witch, Scylla and Charybdis, a female vampire, a smothering python or even a well that you are in danger of falling into — anything, in fact, that is 'female' (in the broadest of senses), but threatening, destroying and/or overwhelming. A brief look into any well-translated book of fairy tales will reveal these, and many other, images of the great mother.

Note that, once again, the archetype has both positive and negative aspects. It must have, because this is a true reflection of human nature. The great mother is also often seen as being quite overwhelming (physically and emotionally). This, at least in part, is a reflection of the fact that the great mother archetype is most significant for us when we are very young. Hence, she is likely to be associated with real-life memories of being physically very small and emotionally very vulnerable. A good example of this sort of thing is the story 'Jack and the Beanstalk', in which Jack (representing the developing ego) is magically transported into a land (the unconscious) where 'everything is just like home but much larger' and where a terrible giant and his wife live.

It is impossible, in part of a single chapter, to do justice to all the ramifications of the great mother in our dreams. These, after all, will represent, at different times and in different people, everything that mothers can be, all the multiple variations of the mother-complex and the development of the relationship between the ego and the great mother that occurs as we grow up. However, we can look briefly at some of the more common and important themes.

As noted above, a small child is likely to have an attitude of adoration of and submission to the inner great mother. And it will, if it is in any way possible (and, often, in the face of quite awful behaviour on the part of the real-life mother), try with all its might to project all of the positive aspects of the great mother onto the real parent so that it can love her and depend on her. Even when a child has a physically abusive and unloving mother it will see her as really loving and worthy of worship, or, if the worst comes to the worst, it will invent (or dream about) a 'good mummy, who loves me' who, perhaps, only comes out when the real mother is asleep, or who lives in the child's dreams. This is a necessary protective device, so that the child can feel a positive relationship with the symbol of the inner great mother archetype: it is necessary for mental health and is only challenged at great risk to the child. Hence, the confusion of many adults who still have dreams of loving parental images that, so far as they know, never existed. These dreams may represent either very selective memories from early childhood or a continuing effort by the unconscious to create an inner happy childhood to compensate for the lack of one in real life. This is a proper and positive attempt at psychological balance and should never be dismissed as mere 'wishful thinking'.

As we grow up, though, our adoration of our 'perfect mother' will eventually have to end, so that we can become self-sufficient adults. It would seem that one of the commonest ways of beginning to break the stranglehold of the perfect mother is to begin (unconsciously) to project the negative rather than the positive aspects of the great mother onto our real-life mother. Instead of a perfect mother, we have a wicked stepmother or a wicked witch in the house! Fairy stories such as 'Cinderella' or 'The Beautiful Wassilissa' are good illustrations of the sort of process involved.

An adult who has dreams about an overwhelmingly powerful, negative female being should always consider the possibility of the presence of still unresolved negative mother-images from childhood. Again, as with 'perfect mother' imagery, this is not at all unusual. Many children, especially those who are not sufficiently helped to develop independently in the world, find it emotionally impossible to give up their worship of the perfect mother (and its associated ongoing identification with childhood roles). Others are so horrified to 'find' that their mother is also a 'wicked witch' that they never confront this problem, relegate it to the unconscious and have nightmares about the witch for the rest of their lives. The answer, as illustrated in any fairy story worth its salt, is (psychologically) to leave the security of the parental home and childhood roles and to venture into the forest of the unconscious and there to confront and debate with the witch in her hut. In other words, to confront one's own unconscious imagery and get to know it. If this is done successfully, the growing child will return home out of the forest, and find it changed and occupied by a harmless old couple with whom it is possible to live a normal life (the real-life parents minus great-parent projections). Independence and marriage are likely to follow shortly (at any age). In chapter seven we saw how many of these themes — but in relation to the father complex — are worked out in the film *The Silence of the Lambs* and how films and other works of art today have largely replaced the fairy tales of two hundred years ago as carriers of psychological knowledge and patterns.

An important further point needs to be made (and is discussed again in Dream Analysis Rule Ten in chapter fourteen). Many people with unresolved parental complexes, upon discovering that their dream imagery is of this sort, take the problems to the real-life parent (often, by now, in her or his seventies or eighties) in order to 'have it out'. They want to discuss their parenting, their parent–child relationships and how they feel about the parent as a result. Please try very hard not to do this! The result is likely to be a great deal of distress and confusion to an old man or woman, who did their confused, often unconscious, best as a parent, can't remember the events of your childhood in as much detail as you can, and will have no idea what all the psychological terms you use mean. Once we are adults, our parent complexes are ours, not our parents'. Trying to re-involve the parent, in many instances, will turn out to be really an attempt to re-project one's own archetypal images onto a (now reluctant) real-life parent. Listen to the fairy stories. The developing child leaves the parental home to deal with the great mother, on her or his own, in the forest of the unconscious. When this is done the all-good mother and the wicked stepmother (the real mother as seen via archetypal projections) are both gone for ever. Don't try to bring them back!

Another important problem of dream analysis is the way that, for some people, erotic and/or creative dreams involving what 'should' be the anima or animus, actually involve a dream figure who looks distinctly like our father or mother. This can be embarrassing or shameful to the dreamer, but is actually quite common and usually (see also below) represents merely a problem of animus/anima differentiation.

The anima/animus actually differentiates rather slowly in us. And, for almost all of us, the first remembered images of the opposite sex are those of the contrasexual parent. These are taken in long before we have a well-formed anima or animus. As Jung put it, in relation to the mother–son relationship:

The mother is the first feminine being with whom the man-to-be comes in contact, and she cannot help playing, overtly or covertly, consciously or unconsciously, upon the son's masculinity.[5]

Later on, as the anima/animus develops, and as we need to create unconscious imagery of our contrasexual side, these are very likely to be, at first, provided from the stock of parental images. In this sense, the anima/animus may be regarded as evolving from the great mother or great father. Later on, as we grow up, we will have broader and broader experiences of members of the opposite sex, from a huge variety of sources. The anima/animus will become correspondingly filled out with a variety of imagery and it would seem that, with time, the unconscious comes to select those images that are nearest to the 'true' essence of the individual's personal contrasexual side. In the authors' opinion, a well-developed anima/animus image is often of an 'unknown' person of the opposite sex, who seems strangely familiar, but no longer has a strong resemblance to any one real-life person. Don't forget that Dante's Beatrice, perhaps the most famous inspirational anima figure in literature, was an image of a girl, glimpsed briefly and only once by Dante, that continued to develop and act as an inspiration in his inner mind for the rest of his life.

So, if your animus/anima looks too much like your mother or father, it is likely that you still need to differentiate your contrasexual imagery from a still-powerful parental complex. This may require a conscious decision for creative and emotional independence or a journey into the unconscious to take power from the archetypal parent. An example of an anima-cum-great mother dream was experienced by a client in psychotherapy with one of the authors. The dreamer was a 47-year-old, male ex-minister who was experiencing difficulties with his third marriage: all his wives has been older than himself, and apparently all placid, good home-makers. The dream is given here as originally written:

I am at the beach. There are a lot of people about. I notice a very attractive lad of about eight years. There is a woman there. I seem to sense both her presence and danger for the boy. I am very anxious.

Then I find that it is time to leave and everyone seems to be gone. I am standing in the bush and see the body of the boy. He seems quite dead. I pick him up and walk down the hill. As I do so I have an increasing sense of danger. My wife is with me, but she is strangely dressed and looks different somehow. She suddenly points behind and screams out a warning to me.

I look up over my shoulder, and this creature is poised over me. It is greater than human size, with eyes blazing with fury and a huge mouth with long, wicked fangs on either side of the top jaw. Curling round behind it, poised over me and ready to strike, is a scorpion tail with two long, curved spikes. I try to strike it but miss, but it evades me and leaps onto my back. I throw myself backwards — and find that she is gone.

Then my wife comes from behind me and takes my arm. She seems very small. She says, 'Are you all right?' We walk down a path through the bush and are joined by a huge man. He says, 'Is it about the boy?' I say, with a huge struggle, 'He was killed by a foul, stinking...WITCH! I shriek the last words and begin to shout all the foul abuse I can think of. I turn round to look down at my wife and see that she is, in fact, the creature. She rears at me, her right arm going above her head to strike me.

I wake up, shaking with fear and anger.

The first thing to notice in this dream is that the dreamer is aware of himself both as adult and child. Upon discussion, it became clear that he identified both with the 'dream ego' (the 'I' within the dream) and the boy, and that the dead boy represents some part of the dreamer's ego that he felt had been 'murdered' at about the age of eight. Psychologically, this meant that some part of his youthful energy and creativity had ceased to function or grow at this age.

As the dream opens, the scene is one that should represent a happy, social event. Instead, there is a clear realisation that the dreamer, as a boy, is in the presence of a woman who represents danger, who accompanies him and then warns him of danger. When the dreamer turns to face danger, he seems become much younger. Upon further association and analysis it became apparent that he, in fact, 'became' the endangered or dead eight-year-old. The monstrous creature-witch therefore seemed much larger than him. Note also how, in his account, the creature is at first called 'it', but then 'she' as he recognised it as being female. He was unaware of the change until it was pointed out. The dreamer is actually able to fight back at the creature, so that it retreats: and when he picks up his 'dead' younger self, he is showing signs of the ability to take responsibility for and deal with his problem.

A very significant sequence of events now occurs. His 'wife' reappears and again appears to try to assist him. Note that, after his successful struggle with the creature, the wife/anima is diminished in size (she is smaller than in the earlier scene). A huge man (surely representing a male parental image from about the same early period of life) also appears and helps him to express his feeling about the death of his younger self. When he is able to express his rage and hatred, the anima figure reveals itself as actually being the witch-creature (but smaller now, of course) and the dream ends with fear, anger and confrontation.

Upon discussion, the dreamer spontaneously — and with some surprise — realised that the creature strongly 'resembled' his mother, but in some way that he found difficult to put into words. It also seemed possible that the upraised 'sting' actually represented a real memory of being threatened with a smack by his mother. And it became clear that, in his unconscious, the dreamer still felt threatened and actually damaged by the negative, archetypal aspect of the great mother — thirty-nine years after some of the 'events' of the dream. Despite this, the dream has a very positive aspect, as represented by the way in which the dreamer is able to take responsibility for his 'dead' self, to fight back against the mother-complex and to express his rage.

Possibly most fascinating of all is the clear interchangeability of a helpful anima figure that has the face of the dreamer's wife (more-or-less) and the terrifying, negative aspect of the archetypal great mother. The dreamer's anima does help. She warns him of danger, and she takes his arm with apparently real concern. But, at the same time, she is, or contains, or changes into, the witch-creature. She is not truly differentiated from the mother-complex, in other words, and one of the dreamer's most important and immediate tasks is that of separating out the helpful and non-maternal aspects of his anima and giving these an independent existence. The dreamer's real-life mother, incidentally, is a rather pleasant old lady, with whom the dreamer has, at least at the level of ego-consciousness, a 'normal' relationship.

One final point that needs to be discussed further in this chapter is that parental images in dreams may be erotic in nature, or have erotic overtones. Freud took such overtones literally, and assumed that they represent remembered, real childhood sexual desire for one's parents. This approach can have a most unfortunate effect on parent–child relationships! In recent years, by contrast, it has, equally unfortunately, become quite common practice to assume that such images actually represent the presence of sexual abuse by the parent. While, of course, there are a minority of people who seem to have Oedipus or Electra complexes, much as Freud described them, and while, in other cases, such dreams can indeed suggest real sexual abuse, in the great majority of cases these dreams cannot and should not be interpreted in these ways. Dreams, after all, are symbolic representations of the inner world of the dreamer, and their relationship to objective events is, at best, selective.

It is unfortunate that, in our society, close and affectionate relationships are so often seen as limited to sexual encounters. The result is that our warmest feelings for others tend to be 'eroticised' unnecessarily. We think that, if affection is present, there must be a sexual overtone to the relationship. This is, in terms of the natural history of our species, actually unnatural, if we compare such attitudes to those of many societies, including tribal ones, where close, lifelong bonding of members of the same sex may involve a great deal of body contact and exchange of statements of love, without any suggestion of a sexual relationship. In any society, of course, our relationships with our parents are (hopefully) very intimate, with a great deal of affection and body contact. The result of all this, in our society, is that all too frequently when we pass puberty and become sexual beings, and as we come to eroticise all our close relationships, we can also eroticise our relationships with our parents, after the event.

Most responsible therapists, presented with apparently erotic dreams about parent figures, will make both a non-accusatory investigation of the relationship of the dream to real-life events and look for the symbolic meaning of the dreams in the light of the dreamer's needs for love, affection and intimacy. They will also study the relationship, within the dreamer's unconscious, between the ego and archetypal, parental structures (see also Dream Analysis Rule Eleven in chapter fourteen).

In summary, then, the great mother and great father are innate archetypes within every human. More has been written about the former. The great mothers can be symbolised by anything — good or bad — that human mother can be: it must encompass every possibility, so that each child can 'recognise' the archetype in its own mother. Dream images of the great mother encompass everything that is supportive, loving and protective, or threatening and overwhelming. She is often seen as huge and overwhelming and may invoke an attitude of adoration and submission in the dreamer. Positive images of the great mother are necessary to the psychological wellbeing of a very young child and may be 'invented', if life does not provide them, and projected onto the real-life mother. At a later developmental stage, all the negative aspects of the great mother are likely to be projected onto the real mother, who may then be seen as a 'wicked witch' or 'evil stepmother'. 'Infinitely-good' or 'wicked witch' mother dreams in an adult suggest that these (normal) phases of development need to be worked through. This should be done by the dreamer as an internal process, and not by confronting the real-life parent with supposed wrongs. Many people have dreams in which the animus/anima clearly resembles a parent figure: this often suggests the presence of a powerful parent-complex and a problem in evolving an independent, adult contrasexual side. Dreams of parent figures may also have an erotic content that suggest Oedipal or Electral impulses or sexual abuse in infancy. While these possibilities should always be tested against reality, it should also be remembered that, for many people, all affectionate relationships are seen in a sexual light: intimate childhood relationships can, as a result, be eroticised *post-hoc*. When this occurs, a broader understanding of parent–child (and other) affectionate relationships needs to be attempted.

Notes

[1] Johnson, R. 1977. *He: Understanding Masculine Psychology*. New York: Harper & Row.
[2] Bly, R. 1990. *Iron John: A Book about Men*. Shaftesbury, Dorset: Element.
[3] Samuels, A.1985. *The Father: Contemporary Jungian Perspectives*. New York: New York University Press.
[4] Biddulph, S. 1995. *Manhood*. Sydney: Tower Books.
[5] Jung, C. G.1969. *Collected Works*, 9i; 162. Princeton: Princeton University Press.

'There lives a child in all of us ...' *(Photo courtesy Geoff Gore)*

OTHER ARCHETYPES

In addition to our immediate consciousness ... there exists a second psychic system of a collective, universal, and impersonal nature which is identical in all individuals. It consists of pre-existent forms, the archetypes, which can only become conscious secondarily and which give definite form to certain psychic contents.

Carl Jung[1]

The shadow, the animus or anima and the parental archetypes are the archetypes most commonly encountered in dreams. There are many more, however, and a few of the more important of these merit at least a brief mention.

The Child

The archetype of the child represents the eternal child in all of us: that part of the psyche that is eternally young. It may also represent creativity, an attitude of renewal and unused potential. It is usually seen in dreams as a child of the same sex as the dreamer (although for parents who have only children of the opposite sex this may not be the case), but can also be represented by young animals of any sort, angels, elves and so on.

When analysing dreams involving the child archetype, one should pay attention to the appearance, the condition and the associated feelings of this image. They may tell us a great deal about our attitude towards our own potential and creativity. Thus, dreams of a starving, sick or dead child may suggest the lack of a healthy use of this part of the psyche. A roomful of starving children may suggest the need for urgent attention to the inner child (see also chapter twelve). A healthy, newly born child in a dream may suggest a new direction for creativity, and so on.

The initial purpose of the child archetype appears to be to help in the establishment of the parent-child bond. When the infant bonds to the mother by projecting on her the great mother archetype, the mother will respond by projecting her archetypal inner child onto the infant. Each then accepts the other's projection — the infant by identifying with the archetypal child, the mother by accepting the identity of the great mother (this latter is almost irresistible, as every mother knows). Mutual projection and acceptance of projected, archetypal roles makes for a close, unconscious bonding. Note that this means we all get two chances to understand our archetypal child: first, when we act out the role in childhood and, second, when we see it in our own children.

The archetypal, inner child is not a real child, of course. It is an all-purpose and numinous mental structure, not a living human. If we want to understand the difference, think of the difference between the way real-life kids behave and the way they are (usually) depicted in literature. The difference is created by the workings of the archetype in the writer. It is the difference between Calvin, of Calvin and Hobbes (one of the most realistic of cartoon children depictions), and the (almost irritatingly perfect, but somehow inhuman) Little Prince in the St Exupery novel of the same name.

The archetype of the inner child is one of the most beautiful and positive of the archetypal energies. But this beauty contains its own danger. It is very easy, when young, to play the role of the archetypal child for all it's worth and to play it too much or too long. We can get caught in identification with the role. This is what happened to Peter Pan — the boy who wouldn't grow up — and to many other 'eternal boys'.

Jung identified two particular pathological manifestations of neurotic identification with the archetypal child. The first is a sense of terrible ill-use and abandonment — of being terribly badly treated and left all alone in the universe. This sort of imagery is found in the plays of John Osborne or of Buechner, for example. The second manifestation is that of the absolutely golden, eternal child, full of a potential beyond the understanding of ordinary mortals (for example, our parents) and of being somehow magically — even divinely — gifted (despite all the evidence to the contrary). Repeated dreams of dramatically ill-used or magnificent children may suggest the presence of a problem with growing away from an unhappy identification with the archetype of the child. For those interested in this archetype, we would recommend Jung's essay on the subject.[2]

The Hero/Heroine

One of the commonest themes in myths and fairy stories is that of the hero (and, nowadays, also the heroine), who goes on a journey — to become king, or solve the insoluble problem, or rescue the maiden, or whatever. Briefly, hero myths may be taken as representing the 'adventures' of the developing ego as it tries to become 'king of the psyche (or kingdom)', meet with its contrasexual partner and overcome all the complexes (especially parental ones) that are so well represented by dragons and ogres. The patterns of hero myths have been well documented and usually include a humble but mysterious or miraculous birth and early life, an early proof of special properties (the ego is always the 'true king'), an encounter with a wise guide who gives direction, a meeting, struggle and then friendship with a companion of the same sex (symbolising shadow properties), a great deed that is to be done for the general good (often involving a struggle with thinly disguised parental images) and the achievement of anything from kingship (in the Arthurian legends) to coming to be the first light of dawn (in the Mickmack Indian tradition). After successful achievement may come overweening pride, the fall of the hero through some little, overlooked weakness, and a death that is somehow redemptive, or consolidates, the great deed: all of which is often considered to represent the need to resubmerge a dominating ego into the psyche as a whole in the second half of life (see also chapter twelve). Most of the story structures above will be found in hero myths, from those about Gilgamesh, Achilles and Sampson, through to others about Arthur and Parsifal, to Luke Skywalker. For those interested in the subject, we would recommend Joseph L. Henderson's article in *Man and His Symbols*[3] and an analytic viewing of the *Star Wars* series.

In analysis today, heroic dreams seem to be rather unusual. At least, one is seldom aware, while in a dream, that one is playing the role of the hero. One is far too well aware of how frightened or miserable one is and how terrifying the dragon is. But, when we make love with a partner or manage not to be killed by a dragon, we would, very often, look heroic to an outsider. We are actually more often aware of our inner hero-ego in our fantasies and daydreams when we are going through a major life-change or experiencing a vividly heroic event and only notice that we sometimes play the same roles in our dreams. An example of such a dream is given in chapter thirteen.

The Trickster

The archetype of the trickster represents everything inside us that wants to upset and overturn rules, morality, and prevailing order in general. It is the inner iconoclast — the mischievous voice that makes us laugh in the middle of the most pompously serious sermon or to want to break up things so that something new can emerge. The last phrase gives us the purpose of trickster activity. It represents the human instinct not to let things get too settled, not to lose our creativity and changeability. It is seen in such figures as the Greek Mercurius, Mr Punch, the circus clown, Tom Thumb and carnivalia in general; in farce and much of comedy, the plays of writers such as Joe Orton and Henry Fielding, and films and TV series such as *Wayne's World* and some episodes of *The Simpsons*; and in those public figures and friends who always seem to be joking and generally opposing current values. One of the most famous examples of the last type of character was the comedian Peter Cook. One of the funniest men ever produced by England, and something of a creative genius to whom the satirical movements of the sixties and beyond owed an enormous debt, he was a man whose determination to mock and undermine established values so dominated his life that he never became known as a 'serious' actor or writer. By wholeheartedly living out so many of the characteristics of a single archetypal pattern, he became — in the eyes of most of the world — a 'failure'. He never achieved fame in other fields, or much wealth, that is, but his influence on British social change over two decades was, in our opinion, very great.

Another good example appears in the 1991 comedy *Drop Dead Fred*. Despite poor reviews, for our purposes this film is redeemed by its psychological value! After a traumatic separation from her husband, the 'heroine' (played by Phoebe Cates) returns home to the domineering influence of her mother. At this point Fred (Rik Myall) appears — a chaotic, destructive imaginary friend from her childhood. A mixture of child, animus and trickster energy, Fred 'assists' in creating an environment where her new, more mature and independent self can emerge, free from the constraints of mother, society and ex-spouse, by constantly destroying the status quo, offending and ridiculing figures of authority and the 'proper' way of doing anything. Having served this purpose, Fred, quite rightly, as one would expect of this form of energy, then disappears.

Trickster energy demands an outlet in every society and individual. In the theocratic societies of medieval Europe, for example, there were 'fools'

Clown on a trapeze steals an actors mask (Photo by David Haynes)

feasts that resembled saturnalia, with 'fool's popes' presiding within the church over wild and shameless release of all sorts of appetites. The church itself was well aware of the need for this periodic release. In the individual dream, the trickster may be experienced as a seductive or tempting figure that gets one into trouble, or simply as the experience of normally forbidden places, acts or feelings. The relationship of the trickster to compensation for over-sober waking attitudes is obvious. The benefit to the dreamer may be that the appearance of the trickster is a reminder that some conscious attitude or behaviour has become over-rigid and over-identified with virtue, and that, in the interests of psychological growth, we may need to let go of it. The end result of trickster activity should always be a rearrangement of attitudes and other psychic properties, to help the individual to move on.

Death or The Night Journey: The Inner Journey

The theme of a journey is very common in dreams and may symbolise changes (mental 'journeys') of all kinds, or even simply the sense of ongoing journeying that is a part of being alive. The term 'night journey' is usually reserved for dreams that relate to the sort of situation where the ego needs to be submerged within the unconscious in order to be renewed. We may need to lose existing structures and attitudes (and complexes) to become more healthy, or to move from one major life-phase to another, for example. This is often experienced in dreams as being swallowed up by some monster, or as a terrible journey into the underworld, or even as death — to be followed by a sense of renewal or the discovery of a house or church in which one may now live or, at the least, an emergence into a land that has been renewed. Well-known examples of the theme include Jonah and the whale, the journeys of Orpheus and Odysseus into the underworld. The theme also underpins some of the most important parts of Christianity. At a more personal level, one of the authors experienced a major change in spiritual direction after a dream in which he allowed himself (after much struggle) to fall down the slope of a volcano into the terrible crater below. The crater turned out to contain a beautiful copse of trees, within which was a 'personal' chapel.

A word of warning at this point. A dream of death or being overwhelmed should not always be taken to suggest the presence of impending healthy growth. While inner renewal very often involves a sense of being overwhelmed, the reverse is not always true. A sense of this, rather, may suggest incipient neurosis or even psychosis. It is all a matter of whether the ego is strong enough to deal with the unconscious material involved and is ready for growth, rather than struggling to contain a flood of material. In particular, repeated dreams of death or being overwhelmed unrelieved by a development towards renewal, escape or growth, always suggest that help should be sought (see also Dream Analysis Rule Three in chapter fourteen).

A less overwhelming but related and common theme in dreams is that of the 'inner journey'. In this, the dreamer goes on a long journey, often by rather strange means, into unfamiliar, often wild, country. Typically, the later stages of the journey are undertaken alone or on foot. We have seen a variant of this dream in a number of our own Australian clients in which the journey has led into the Australian outback and ended at a lake or pool of water that contains fish. A variant of this theme is where the dreamer 'discovers' a strange but familiar house and explores it, perhaps finding unknown floors or rooms (symbolising hitherto unknown unconscious contents). Just such a dream was experienced by Jung as a young man and assisted him in his understanding of the nature of the collective unconscious.[4] Whatever the variation, dreams of this sort turn out, very often, to be an exploration of one's own psyche, with the different rooms, or stages of the journey representing different aspects of the mind. The endpoint of the journey, may represent either the deepest level to which consciousness can penetrate or a new, often unexpected, central image that demands attention. The Christian imagery, the absence of containing structures and the naturalness of the Australian example is very striking and strongly suggest a potential for renewal in the Australian psyche. No general rules for interpretation of dreams having journey motifs can be given, but dreams of the inner journey often provide, at the very least, the opportunity to look at some of your 'inner landscape' and wonder at the complexity, the number of rooms, the length of the journey and the extraordinary beauty, complexity and oddity of the images and their juxtapositions.

The Wise, Old Person

In almost every major myth, as the heroes go on their journeys, eventually they will meet with an apparently insignificant old person. If they treat the old man or woman courteously and kindly, the latter will give them some mysterious but invaluable advice, or a magical object perhaps, which will prove invaluable at a later stage of the journey. For example, a box that appears empty, but contains a spirit that can move mountains, or a sword that can kill an ogre that has yet to appear. This theme represents the way that the ego, if it treats the unconscious psyche with respect, will receive all sorts of help and wisdom when it is least expected. Perhaps it will find that it can use a hitherto neglected attitude or that lunchtimes are better spent painting or reading poetry rather than catching up on one's mail.

Jung used the term 'wise old man' to describe such figures, and considered them to be an (unconscious) 'guru' or wise person, who would appear when good advice, understanding, insight and so on was needed, guiding the ego onto the right path, but often doing so by giving the ego a problem to solve rather than simply pointing the way.[5] The wise old man is also commonly believed to point the way to individuation and the self and perhaps to be, in some major way, a part of the latter.

Dreams involving unexpected help or advice from an older person are just as common in modern Australians as in literature. But, in our experience, there has been a development over the last couple of decades. Where, in the literature, the older person encountered is almost always a wise old man, Australian women today are more likely to get their advice from a wise old woman. (Shirley Maclean in a cave or Governor Roma Mitchell on the banks of the river Torrens, are two recent examples.) The wise old person has become gender-liberated, as the concept that a women cannot have a completely free and independent ego has begun to evaporate.

The Persona

The persona, or mask, is a term for an archetypal ability that helps our socialisation, particularly at a fairly superficial level. Like the ego, the idea of the persona is a psychological concept that is generally accepted. The persona, then, is the 'public face' that we wear when in the presence of others. It helps us relate to others without having to be too exact or think too carefully about what we are saying and whether this reflects our 'true' self. It is a convenient social shell, in other words. Or, rather, a series of shells, because almost everyone has a number of personae, each adapted to a different situation. If you doubt this, try to remember times when you have found someone boring and/or rigid because they seemed to be the same in every situation!

The persona is almost the opposite of the shadow. It is relatively unemotional, not emotionally powerful and primitive; socially acceptable, not the reverse; and on the surface of the psyche, not lurking in the depths. And it is as important for the ego to be aware of the presence of the persona, and not to be over-identified with it, as also in the case of the shadow. Too close an identification with the persona is commonly held to lead to superficiality, a sense of a lack of 'true' feeling and a loss of contact with the deeper layers of the psyche (a problem that is discussed again in the next chapter).

We seem to dream about the persona most vividly when we are afraid that it is being lost — that people will be able to see behind our social mask. Dreams of being naked in public (sometimes while sitting on the lavatory) or of all our teeth falling out are often of this sort. Our beautiful clothing is lost and people will be able to see all the shit inside us! Sometimes dreams can be very direct and ungenteel.

Notes

[1] Jung, C. G. 1969. *Collected Works*, 9i; 90. Princeton: Princeton University Press.
[2] Jung, C. G. 1969. *Collected Works*, 9i; 259–304. Princeton: Princeton University Press.
[3] Henderson, J. 1964. Ancient myths and modern man. In C.G. Jung and M.-L. von Franz (eds), *Man and His Symbols*. London: Aldus.
[4] Jung, C. G. 1995. *Memories, Dreams, Reflections*. London: HarperCollins. pp. 182–8.
[5] Jung C. G. 1969. *Collected Works*, 9i; 398–9. Princeton, NJ: Princeton University Press.

'Origins' *(Lino print Katrina Tierney-Smith)*

12
THE SELF

Therefore, as it seems, it is the greatest of all disciplines to know oneself; for when a man knows himself, he knows God.

Clement of Alexandria[1]

You may have noted, in the last chapter, that certain of the archetypes relate to particular life stages or to problems connected with specific ages or stages of development. This is certainly the case, and in this chapter we will attempt to relate archetypal motifs, in dreams and elsewhere, to the healthy development of the human mind and spirit — first, by giving an account of healthy psychological development in Jungian terms, and, second, by looking at possible patterns of spiritual growth from other disciplines.

The Jungian Concept of Healthy Development

In Jungian theory, healthy lifelong development is a natural process of growth that will always take place and be self-generating given a sound psychological, social and spiritual environment. The usual overall pattern, at least in our society, has two phases. A pattern of growth, extroversion and world-relatedness — the 'years of the ego' — in the first half of life, and a pattern of inner work, centring and spiritual development in the second half of life, which should be regarded as largely a preparation for death. In all of this, the relationship between the ego and the 'self' is of the greatest importance. The meaning of the word 'self', though, in Jungian terms, needs explanation.

The Jungian concept of the 'self' refers to a central, guiding archetype at the core of the psyche. This gives purpose, direction and structure to lifelong development. Some Jungians tend to think of the self as having or containing a sort of blueprint for the individual's unique developmental path. A conscious encounter with the self can be an overwhelming experience that can even lead to psychosis — very much like a too-direct or over-long encounter with God in the Scriptures. Jung would have said, though, that while descriptions of the self sound very much like descriptions of God, or at least a god, it isn't the job of psychology to speculate about the nature of this resemblance. Rather, it is the task of psychology to describe the nature of the self as honestly as possible, as though it were a psychic structure. If, then, what we term the central archetype is modelled on, or a pathway to, an external God, this merely emphasises our need for an (ego-) attitude of honesty and respect when dealing with an entity that is so much greater than ego-consciousness.

One of the central problems of psychological development, according to Jung, is the separation between ego and self that is the experience of the great majority of people. The ego is said to be, at birth, inseparable from the self: the two coexist. But, as the individual grows up — at least in modern society — it is necessary that the ego evolve into an independent and powerful entity responsible for our dealings with the world, our thinking and decision-making, our political views, and so on. A split of the ego-self connection (or 'axis', as Jung called it) is inevitable and the original relationship is 'remembered' as a sense of union and harmony that has been lost.

Two problems arise. First, if the ego-self split is too great, the ego will be split off from the source of most of the unconscious energy of the psyche — from the most powerful emotions and the major archetypes. It will become de-energised. And, because the self seems to be the centre or source of spiritual life, it will split off from spirituality as well. A crisis may then occur (maybe a 'mid-life crisis'), as the ego becomes unable to sustain an arid existence. The individual will have to give up a degree of ego-control and look back into the psyche in an attempt to reconnect with the self. Often this involves dealing with the shadow (see also below). The second problem is that, regardless of the extent of the ego-self split, every individual will discover a need for a stronger ego-self axis in the second half of life. Once past the mid-way point of life, success in the ego-world has less and less meaning, as one becomes more and more aware that one's physical energies are diminishing and that one needs to be preparing for the death that is the end-point of this phase of life. Jung himself often said that he had never had a patient in the second half of life whose central need was not to find a spiritual attitude to existence. Ego-self (of, if you like, individual-God) reconciliation becomes for everyone the driving force in the second half of life.

Let us now look at this developmental pattern in a little more detail, and bring in a few more archetypes. To begin with, the ego of the small child is immersed in the self, from which it has yet to be differentiated. The first step in this differentiation comes with recognition of the mother, the projection of the great mother archetype onto the real-life mother and the consequent identification of the personality with the archetype of the child. Adoration of the mother and (probably) mother complexes develop at this point, with father complexes perhaps following soon after.

After a few years, the ego will need to emerge from the parental complexes. This generally follows the pattern described in chapter ten, with the projection of negative aspects of the mother and father archetypes onto the respective parents. The all-good mother and father 'die' and the wicked witch and ogre/giant are born. The ego then begins its identification with the hero archetype by, hopefully, venturing into the dark forest of the unconscious and there meeting with the archetypal witch-ogre. When it returns, if all has gone well, the witch or ogre projection onto the real parents should have been banished and the parents will be seen as just ordinary people.

At this point, the anima or animus will be able to emerge from the initial parental imago: just as, at this point in the fairy story, Prince Charming or Sleeping Beauty appear or are woken up, and the individual begins to deal with his or her contrasexual side. If the individual can gain some knowledge of this contrasexual side before puberty, then falling in love — the projection of anima/animus onto a member of the opposite sex — may not be quite as uncontrolled and devastating an experience as might otherwise be the case. The ego is now strongly identified with the myth of the hero, having overcome ogres and witches and courted the lovely princess/prince. Heroic (and sometimes desperate) attitudes are likely as study, career, marriage, parenthood and other 'dragons' have to be slain.

During all this period, the individual has been making life choices and selecting personality characteristics, and, by definition, building up a stronger and stronger unconscious shadow personality that, more commonly than not, is more and more ignored. Spiritual development, involving as it does humility and the setting aside of ego boundaries, is also quite likely to be resolutely repressed in many people. Physical, social and material development seem to be enough and life is controlled by an ego–persona alliance.

Then, one morning, the individual wakes up and is forty-five years old. The old decisions and the reliance upon things of the ego won't do any more and the persona is seen for the insubstantial thing that it is. The problem is that twenty years of one-sided but consistent decisions and development can't be reversed in a short time, if at all. Individuals, in order to begin to develop towards the rediscovery of wholeness, must go back, at least to puberty and often to early childhood, if they are to discover what remains of all those parts of themselves that were never developed and the pathways they never took. Usually they are aware of a profound dissatisfaction that may affect every aspect of life, or of a terrible sadness and yearning for the past — often a past that is only vaguely (and often inaccurately) remembered, but which is felt to have contained a sense of hope, or wholeness, or joy, or creativity, or even simplicity that seems to be missing from their present existence. And, usually, they have no idea what to do about it.

The danger at this point is that the individual will decide that the task — if there is indeed such a thing — is too hard, or too silly, or too socially or financially unacceptable, and give up, instead trying to be satisfied with what inevitably becomes a shrinking life, with diminishing rewards and satisfactions. It is difficult to find a book about mid-life change written by a Jungian that does not spell out the necessity for the abandonment of long-established ego attitudes and to find an alternative way of existence that is genuinely not just a disguised version of the old one. Readers are recommended Peter O'Connor's *Understanding the Midlife Crisis*[2] and *Coming to Age* by Jane Pretat[3] for two excellent discussions of this issue.

There are no general rules about using one's dream material in the search for renewal and spiritual growth. Everyone's path has been different and no two people have precisely the same innate nature. The reader is strongly advised to avoid books and other publications that claim to have universal rules and guidelines. Neither is it the job of psychology to tell people which direction to go. Spiritual growth means different things to different people and everyone, in the end, is solely responsible for the direction he or she takes. All that the authors can do is outline, and give some examples of, the commonest situations, conflicts and outcomes that they have experienced or observed over the years.

Transitions of Spiritual/Faith Development

In addition to the Jungian model above, a number of researchers in a variety of disciplines have attempted to chart human development. Kohlberg and other social psychologists, for example, initiated work on aspects of moral development. James Fowler, in *Stages of Faith* [4], sought to describe a series of maturing stages of faith, and many other people have since developed and revised these early models. Harold Grant explored the development of personality type and ageing. In recent years, some of these conclusions and research has been called into question, particularly by feminist writers. For example, Fowler's work has some clear cultural and historical limitations. Notwithstanding such critique, what is of interest for our purposes is that most, if not all of this research, has a basic agreement that in middle life (thirty-five years onwards), we are most likely to see a rekindling or renewing of interest in the spiritual dimension of life, *if such issues have not already been addressed healthily.*

In *From image to likeness*[5], Harold Grant and his colleagues present a description of spiritual wholeness that some may find helpful. Grant describes a strong link between personal development and spiritual wholeness. Wholeness is described in terms of the degree to which a person develops the power or freedom to exercise each of her or his personality attributes in accordance with the call of each of life's situations, and the degree to which all aspects of personality are exercised in harmony, though not without an emerging and creative tension.

Wholeness is reached through the developmental stages of the life journey. It is not inevitable (it has to be worked for) and it does not happen in isolation, but in community.

Finally, even the negative dimensions and expressions of personality and environment can become food for growth (so that avoidance of pain and suffering is not the pathway, or goal, of wholeness).

It is important to note that in none of these models is there any inevitability to the process and that, while they are framed chronologically, a person may jump stages, revisit them at a later time etc. These are dynamic, not static, models.

For those from strong evangelical traditions, it is important to understand that Fowler, for example, understood conversion experiences as experiences that changed the *content* of faith. Conversion is:

> ... *a significant re-centering of one's previous conscious or unconscious images of value and power, and the conscious adoption of a new set of*

master stories in the commitment to reshape one's life in a new community of interpretation and action.[6]

Conversion experiences and numinous encounters can, therefore, occur in any of the faith stages. In terms of faith development, it is especially important to recognise that the stages and conversion experiences are independent. A conversion may initiate change, but changes often happen without them, perhaps through a particular circumstance in which we find ourselves. Likewise, a conversion experience may happen without a 'stage' change. A stage change may precipitate a conversion experience, and, paradoxically, a numinous experience may serve to block or limit personal and spiritual development. For example, depending on how we *interpret* an experience, we may feel encouraged and empowered to change something in our lives *or* we might feel overwhelmed by the experience and fail to develop any application of the experience.

Additionally, and of particular interest when we also consider human development from a Jungian perspective, conversion experiences may act as a catalyst for a recapitulative process, whereby we revisit unresolved issues from the past. We may observe that often the issues for personal development in a particular phase of life have a relationship to our faith development. For example, dealing with some of the issues that emerge in the second half of life, such as withdrawing anima/animus projections, may necessitate a change in faith outlook as well as personal responsibility, and recognition of our own persona and projections clearly require a degree of maturity with respect to personal and spiritual development.

Our psychological development, then, works hand in hand with our faith development — if we are committed to the task. While growth and maturity are said, in these developmental theories, to flow quite naturally, we need to recognise that they may be short-circuited at any point. The models above are dynamic models of life, even though they appear somewhat two dimensional when expounded as theories. Thus, we can easily live our entire lives in one of the early stages of development, consciously and unconsciously resisting the call of the self, and the call of God, to continue to grow in self-knowledge and in grace.

The Self and the God-Image

As the self archetype is the central unifying symbol of the psyche, encounters with it bear a close resemblance to those with what people from religious traditions would call God. The existence of the self is not a 'proof' for the existence of a God *per se*, but, rather, experiences of the self have all the qualities of what we would call religious experiences. There is a numinous, mystical quality clearly evident. Dreams in which an encounter with the self occurs have a mystery and power of their own — and the symbols of the self can be varied. They may be an image of Jesus or a mythical god or being, or perhaps of someone who is very famous, or even of a child.

> *It is only through the psyche that we can establish that God acts upon us, but we are unable to distinguish whether these actions emanate from God or from the unconscious. We cannot tell whether God and the unconscious are two different entities.*[7]

What do we make of this? If we are operating from a religious or faith standpoint, we may attach deep religious and 'divine' significance to the encounter. Such a position needs to be respected and affirmed. If we are coming from a non-religious perspective, we might see self-encounters within the framework of personal self-awareness. Edinger, for example, is said to have described the self as the 'organ of acceptance'.[8]

From either standpoint, the self is clearly something that is bigger than the ego, and meeting it is an experience in which the ego is humbled. (It is important to remember that one of the dangers of over-identification with the self is the development of an inflated ego: we may begin to behave as if *we* are God!). This is not a case of one view being right and the other wrong, rather, our initial faith disposition will influence what we make of such experiences.

From a religious standpoint, though, the self may well be seen as a gateway to our experience of God, and a theology with an emphasis on incarnation (God with us), or Orthodox theology with its concept of divinisation, would affirm this: the self being the place where the human and the Divine overlap.

Jung had a particular interest in the story of Job. As Edinger explains in his book *Encounter with the Self*[9], the story serves as a paradigm for the process of individuation. At the same time, it is a paradigm of what we might also call 'conversion', and the experience will be familiar to many religious people. As such, it can be a powerful paradigm for both Christian and non-Christian alike.

First, there is an encounter with an ego and the self/God/superior state

(Job and God); second, a wound is received (Job's afflictions); third, there is perseverance and an exploration of wounding that seeks to discover meaning (the conversations with all Job's 'helpers'); and, finally, there is a revelation or insight that assists the development of the ego, and leads to greater integration, both inwardly and outwardly.

Here we see a pattern of encounter that occurs for many people, even though we may attach slightly different meaning and significance to similar events. It would seem that the self is indeed one of the critical and most important archetypes and paradigms that enables us to grow personally and spiritually.

In the following chapter, we will trace some of these patterns of development by examining several dreams and their meanings. In this way, we will see the practical linking of these theories to people's lives.

Notes

1. Jung, C. G. 1958. *Modern Man in Search of a Soul*. London: Routledge. p. 43.
2. O'Connor, P. 1981. *Understanding the Mid-Life Crisis*. Melbourne: Mandarin.
3. Pretat, J. R. 1994. *Coming to Age: The Croning Years and Late-Life Transformation*. Toronto: Inner City.
4. Fowler, J. W. 1981. *Stages of Faith: The Psychology of Human Development and the Quest for Meaning*. New York: HarperCollins (Collins Dove).
5. Grant, W. H., Thompson, M. & Clarke, T. E. 1983. *From Image to Likeness: A Jungian Path in the Gospel Journey*. Ramsey, NJ: Paulist Press. p. 180.
6. Fowler, J. W. 1981. *Stages of Faith: The Psychology of Human Development and the Quest for Meaning*. New York: HarperCollins (Collins Dove). pp. 281–2.
7. Jung C. G. 1969. *Collected Works*, 11; 757. Princeton, NJ: Princeton University Press.
8. Clift, J. D. & Clift, W. B. 1989. *Symbols of Transformation in Dreams*. Melbourne: Collins Dove. p. 134.
9. Edinger, E. 1986. *Encounter with the Self*. Toronto: Inner City.

Into the wilderness *(Photo by Steve Price)*

STEPS OF THE LIFE JOURNEY THROUGH DREAMS

Dear God, when we fall let us fall inwards. Let us fall freely and completely: that we may find our depth and humility: the solid earth from which we may rise up and love again.

Michael Leunig[1]

Following on from the previous chapter, let us now look at how some of the issues of growth, psychological and spiritual, may be portrayed in dreams.

The first thing that needs to be stated is that, in a full analysis, every facet of the individual's unconscious functioning, including all her or his major conflicts, is likely to be observed at one time or another. This is especially true in periods of crisis (see also Dream Analysis Rule Six in chapter fourteen). While fascinating for a therapist or guide, this tends to be rather confusing and even discouraging for the dreamer, especially when signs of a clear, positive outcome are hard to find. How can one start to sort it all out?

First, by paying particular attention to 'beginning dreams'. These may be dreams that caused the individual to think about dreamwork in the first place. Or they may be dreams that occur within a few days after one decides to begin inner work — typically, in therapeutic practice, dreams that occur between making an appointment to work with someone and the first session. Beginning dreams are quite likely to tell us, in symbolic language, the nature of the problem that is being brought up for investigation.

Two Beginning Dreams

The first dream is from a woman who came into therapy for advice about 'starting a new life after her divorce'. She had recently moved out of home with a lover and stated that her marriage was dead and boring (not necessarily in that order):

> *I was standing in my front garden [of the house shared with the husband]. I seemed to be looking at the house from a new angle, or in a sort of new way — I'm not sure. The house seems to be on a steep hillside, which it isn't in life. I suddenly notice that water is flowing out of the foundations. There is a flood! I can't see where it is coming from but I'm sure it is going to wash away the foundations. I go round the side of the house to investigate. Somehow I can go down along the house at the level of the foundations. I can see the flood waters emerging. It's funny, they seem to be far less than I'd thought. They are coming out of a pipe or a hole in the ground — perhaps a small, underground stream. When I look I can see that they have done only superficial damage to the house: washed away a bit of paint — that sort of thing. The foundations are actually unharmed. I go to ring up a plumber to fix the pipe.*

As soon as the associations of this dream were discussed, it became apparent that the house symbolised the woman's life with her husband. The stream of underground water was, for her, a flood of emotion (a common, but not at all universal meaning for water in dreams) that seemed to be washing away the foundations of her married life — the sexual energy of her affair, it would seem. Upon inspection, though, the flood is seen to be rather unthreatening. The house stands solid. The marriage, it appears, is not going to be lost. When she had a close look at the situation, all she actually needed was a 'plumber' (clearly, if not flatteringly, the therapist) to plug up the flood of emotions. The client was actually unconsciously saying that all she needed was short-term therapy to enable her to control her feelings, and that, despite her verbal statements, she felt that her marriage was going to endure (as actually turned out to be the case).

There are a couple of other points about the imagery in this dream. First, the house, symbolically the marriage, is being looked at 'from a new angle in a new sort of way' — almost a direct, verbal statement about the way the affair is causing the woman to re-appraise her marriage. The house has also been placed on a steep hillside, as though to emphasise the initial sense of danger to it. Second, whether great or small, the source of the flood is still unknown (except that it flows from underground — surely symbolic of unconscious origins). In other words, the woman has been overwhelmed by unconscious emotion and still doesn't know why. Plugging up the current leak is likely to be only a stop-gap measure unless she can gain the insight and knowledge to understand and control her energies. She will be able to control the effects of this affair, but perhaps not similar eruptions in the future.

The second dream is from a man of forty-four years of age, who was entering Jungian therapy as a part of analytic training:

I was standing on a mountainside in a far country: it looked like India. A few people wandered about. I was by a path and, looking down it saw a woman I know as a friend of the family lying by the path. She seemed much younger than in real life — about fifteen perhaps. I made love to her, without any words or preliminaries: it seemed a natural and expected act. Then the scenery changed to Southern Europe — where I worked for a year or so — and it became dark. I went down to the [Mediterranean] sea and embarked on a boat. After a while, we stopped and I dived down into the water and found a number of stone coffins lying on the sea bed. I brought one up to the shore (which had conveniently arrived for the purpose) and opened the coffin. Inside, instead of the expected rotten body was a beautiful Greek lyre. Shining and tuned. I found that I was able to play it. When I did so, two girls that I had known when I was about fifteen appeared.

This dream has a far more 'archetypal feel' than the first and is predictive of the beginning of a deep, inner exploration. Central to this will be the ego–anima relationship. The dream begins in a strange and distant place, unknown to the dreamer — a part of the psyche with which the conscious ego was unfamiliar, even, so far as could be told, in his dreams. He stands about and doesn't really know what to do, just like most people beginning inner work, until he notices the young girl. She, clearly, is an anima figure and when the dreamer has union with her the dream is able to move on to the next phase. There are three other things worth noting here. First, the dreamer's unconscious puts the face of a family friend, someone known but not with great intimacy, onto the anima figure. Upon discussion, the dreamer stated that he had always felt this woman to be warm, open and positive, but straightforward rather than intellectual (almost the reverse of some of his own personality characteristics). The unconscious has picked, as a positive anima figure, a person upon whom positive, non-ego characteristics have already been projected during social intercourse, and chosen someone who is not too familiar. Too close a familiarity with the woman concerned might have prevented the projection from 'taking'. Second, the anima figure is much younger than both the person it resembles and the dreamer: this suggests strongly that the dreamer has a somewhat juvenile, and therefore less than fully developed, inner anima. Third, the dreamer unites with the anima through sexual intercourse. It should be noted here that, upon waking, the dreamer did not feel sexually aroused, and has not since experienced sexual feelings towards the woman whose face his anima had. All of this means that, in this dream, the sex act is symbolic of a broader union between ego and anima.

Union with the anima now allows the dream to develop further. The scenery changes and actions of deeper significance in relation to the ego-anima relationship occur. Curiously (but not unusually) the movement is apparently both towards the unconscious (it becomes night) and towards the familiar and outer-life related (the scene becomes an exotic, but known country). A symbolic journey into the waters of the unconscious is now undertaken to bring up something perceived as long-dead: not just buried, but in a stone coffin! Instead of corruption there is a beautiful musical instrument all ready to be played. When it is played, aspects of the feminine from about the age of fifteen begin to appear. Note that the new anima figures are about the same age as the transformed family friend at the beginning of the dream. The dream is very much concerned with reworking aspects of the dreamer's anima that were 'buried' at the age of about fifteen and now needed to be reworked and allowed to grow up. The result of this was a profound maturation of the dreamer's attitude towards the feminine in general. Note also the presence of the motif of the night journey and the discovery (very common in dreamwork, but usually a shock to the dreamer) that long-forgotten aspects of the psyche are not dead after all, but alive and tuned for use! Finally, there is also more than a passing resemblance to the myth of Orpheus: in this, the lyre symbolised Orpheus' power to communicate with the animal and plant worlds — the creativity that made him so loved, but which needed the presence of the feminine (Eurydice) to make him fully human.

Shadow and Anima/Animus Dreams

The next two dreams illustrate the sort of problems that often emerge quite early in dream analysis. The first is a not untypical encounter with a shadow figure in the dream of a 24-year-old male. This man was still living in the parental home in an Australian country town, but was about to move interstate to study. He was a very logical and organised person, with very controlled feelings. Consequently, he was popular and much relied on by his friends, but was very awkward with women:

I am in a distant city in a foreign country. It may be New York. I am living in a flat at the top of a skyscraper. I can see my parents' home, down in the street, about a million floors below. I feel dirty and want to take a shower, but find that there isn't one in my flat. I try to get back to my parental home, but find the doors downwards are all blocked. Anyway, it is too far to go. I decide instead to get something to eat. There is no stove or fridge in my flat, but then I find myself in an unknown street in a 'diner': an American one, I think. There are a lot of people there, but I especially notice a Negro sitting some distance away. I know that he is a drug dealer, violent and deadly. I hate him, especially when I see him talking to a couple of girls. He speaks gently about his emotions and they laugh and smile at him. I have to deal with this! I go over and try to strangle him: he falls over and I try to gouge out his eyes. He does not resist, but I get angrier and angrier. I wake up feeling very sad and lonely.

Once again, we have a dream that is set in a far country that symbolises new and/or unknown regions of the psyche. The dreamer is unconsciously anticipating his move away from home and already feels a 'million floors' removed from it. He can't go back, emotionally. However, in his new place he doesn't seem to have any of the ordinary conveniences of life. Upon discussion, his associations with the need for a shower related to moral cleanliness and guidance; his associations with food related to the need for strength and energy. So he knows how to get energy for his independent existence, but not where to get moral guidance.

At this point the dreamer finds himself in a sleazy diner. His associations here were with violent American gangster films. The scene is set for aggressive behaviour. And the person that he notices immediately — you could say, is irresistibly drawn towards — is a shadow figure. Black, but not Aboriginal (and so unknown and exotic) and associated with everything that the dreamer detests (drugs and violence), but also with properties that the dreamer lacks (the ability for gentle emotional expression and relationship with the feminine). And the dream ego absolutely hates him! This is a typical reaction, in our society, to our shadow. Note that the fury and violence is all on the part of the ego. The shadow figure is *perceived* by the dream ego as violent and bad, but there is no actual evidence that this is true (see also the discussion on ego–shadow relationships in chapter eight). All of this is a very strong indication that, to the dreamer, emotional expression and contact with the feminine side is inextricably linked to violence, loss of control (drugs) and negative emotions in general. The task for the dreamer is actually to get to know the shadow figure, so that he can make use of its positive properties. The danger is that, in so doing, he will be overcome by aggressive feelings. All of us have probably come across men who, when they first try to express their feelings, become unbearably aggressive for quite a long time before the positive emotions underneath begin to emerge.

The next dream was experienced by a forty-year-old male who had been doing a good deal of work in the same sort of area. He had overcome initial problems with fear of shadow figures, but was now aware of the need to be able to express feelings at a deeper and more meaningful level.

There is some sort of discussion or group happening. Three women lead the discussion and one of them initiates a new phrase — 'Let's get on with it'. The three girls move on to a lawned slope. I am below with a male friend from long ago. The three girls begin to dance around and masturbate to orgasm. They are laughing and joking and seem to feel very comfortable with themselves and their orgasms are very relaxed. They are smiling etc. and encouraging each other to come. The leading girl says, 'Who's next?' After a pause I say it's probably my turn — after all, this is for my benefit? I move up the slope and the girls surround me. The leader tells me it is my turn to come and encourages me to stroke myself. I am incredibly embarrassed, but tentatively try, but cannot succeed. I feel a sense of failure, disappointment, shame etc. My friend is here too and somehow I am instructed (?) to lie back in all of their arms and let myself go. I feel myself falling forwards — and I fall into this crystal clear water, with sandy patches. I find I can breathe in the water and begin to float and swim through it. The sensation is quite pleasant, but whether it is quite what I am meant to be experiencing, I am not sure.

The dreamer found this dream made him feel scared and tearful, but not sexually aroused. On doing some association work with the dream, he felt strongly that the sexual symbolism in the dream represented intimacy and a capacity for openness and sharing that came so naturally to the women in the dream and therefore, for him, was a feminine property. So, once again, we find the erotic analogy being used as a symbol of sharing and emotion. Note the degree of unconscious horror in which emotional sharing must have been held, for it to visualised as public masturbation!

There is a clear advance in this dream as compared to the last. In the former, emotional expression is blocked by a male shadow figure. In this dream, the masculine is represented only by a single, friendly figure and has no power over 'feminine' emotion. Towards the end of the dream, we also see imagery that moves beyond the sexual analogy, when the dreamer 'lets himself go' and then finds he is able to swim and breathe in an entirely new element. This, surely, is the real world of emotional expression. So strange is it to the dreamer that he sees it as a completely new, and potentially fatal, element (and, perhaps, with water again being used as a symbol of the unconscious and unknown). It is so unfamiliar that he is not sure if he is experiencing what he 'should'. With time and work, hopefully, the water will transform into more recognisable and less frightening emotional experiences.

The Abandoned Child and the Wise Woman

So far, in the dreams described in this chapter and elsewhere, we have seen how beginning dreams can tell the dreamer about his or her future direction, we have seen how first the shadow and then the anima/animus may need to be experienced and allowed to help the ego, and we have seen how the anima/animus can be related to parental complexes. These represent the most common themes encountered early in therapy. The next dream is concerned with a long-standing complex that emerged somewhat later into therapy, involving the archetypes of the child and the wise old person. It also demonstrates, once again, how a dreamer may be seduced by the emotional power of a dream and fail to see clear, alternative messages that are present.

The dreamer was a 32-year-old woman who had come into therapy because of long-standing mild depression. She had been a kindergarten teacher for a number of years, with frequent changes of position, and was about to spend two years in India working for a charity. This last decision seemed to have intensified her depression.

There is a young Indian child lying on the ground, about four years old. She is ugly, with a pock-marked face. I stand by her feeling full of sadness. Suddenly she clutches her stomach in pain and begins to groan: she vomits everywhere and struggles. Then I see a hut behind the child. I go into it looking for help. Inside it is enormous! There are hundreds of children inside, many of them coughing with TB or covered with sores. Quite a few are dead or dying. The noise is terrible. I see an old Indian woman standing outside and I rush out to get her to help. She says, 'You cannot help. Leave them alone.' I grab her by the arm, shouting, 'You should go and see how people live.' But somehow she slips away. I go to follow her, but a child in the hut starts to shout, 'Don't leave us!' I don't know what to do.

This dream is an extremely vivid depiction of the abandoned and abused aspect of the archetype of the child. The images are of extreme deprivation and pain and their importance to the dreamer is emphasised by their large number. One should also note that the children are foreign (somewhat alien to the dreamer) and 'ugly' — a vivid image of her attitude to her inner child. Note also that the dreamer was unable to do anything to help (a theme that recurred in a number of dreams with similar imagery). She was stuck!

Upon discussion, it was apparent that the sense of awful abuse of, and neediness in, this woman's inner child had influenced her choices of career and a sense of futility within that career that had led to her many changes of job. She was now 'upping the bets', as it were, by actually going to a 'foreign land' to work with genuinely needy children. By so doing, she was unconsciously trying to make her own inner child feel better. This motivation in her work is what is often referred to as a 'shadow motivation', whereby an unconscious attempt to deal with one's own problems actually underpins a conscious, overt and 'reasonable' job choice: the super-efficient nurse, whose competence masks a fear of ever being ill and helpless, the evangelical social worker whose home life is in chaos, and so on. Shadow motivations, which are especially common in the helping professions (clergy please note!) are beautifully described in Adolf Guggenbuhl-Craig's *Power in the Helping Professions*.[2] Actually, shadow motivations can be a great help — when their significance is clearly understood by their owner. There is nothing wrong with helping our own development via our job, provided that we are aware that this is what we are doing. It will help our motivation and ability to empathise with those who resemble our inner needy part. But if we are unaware of, or deny, our shadow motivation we may be worse than useless. We will mistake inner pain for sympathy and fail to really see those who we are supposed to help because we are really looking at ourselves. The shadow motivation will take over everything and our ability to be objective will be lost.

The other important message from this dream is carried by the 'old Indian woman' — who tells the ego personality to stop trying to help the children. She was right. The dreamer had had a number of jobs caring for children, but had been neither effective in, or made to feel better by, any of them. Hence, the drifting from job to job and the desperate attempt to work with some of the most archetypally needy children in the world. She would have done better to stick with inner work until the inner child was healthy enough *not* to dominate her inner life.

Of course, she would hear none of it: the abandoned inner child was too seductive, so she went off to India, where she spent two miserable years and came back thoroughly disillusioned. It was not until she had completed another year of inner work that she began to break free from the tyranny of her inner abandoned child. At this point she lost all interest in both charity work and Indians, but became an effective teacher! Note also, in this dream, how the wise, old woman drifts in and out of the dream, delivering her message, but is otherwise unnoticeable. This is quite typical of the way that wisdom and advice have always been presented in dreams, myths and fairy stories. The wise, old person can be the most self-effacing of all the archetypal motifs.

The Night Journey and Transformation

We have just seen an example of how, when the dream ego neglects the advice of a wise, old person, it may remain in bondage to an archetypally based complex for a long time. In our final example, we will look at a dream where guidance and advice were absolutely forced on the dream ego and a (long overdue and very important) positive outcome was consequently arrived at far more quickly. The renewal and change seen in the dream below was reflected in a rapid change in the attitudes and mental health of the dreamer: so rapid indeed, that therapy could be positively terminated almost immediately!

The dreamer was a 48-year-old man, an ex-lay preacher who had been in therapy for about a year. His initial reason for entering therapy had been the impending break-up of his third marriage. He had a history of frequent job changes and altercations and arrived discontented and unsatisfied with life. His dreams had been full of fights and chases, full of sound and fury, but actually without major damage to the parties concerned. Usually he was engaged in a running combat with shadowy male figures, often while in search of, or protecting, an equally shadowy female figure. For the past sixth months he had been attempting active imagination with shadow and anima figures, apparently without success. We say apparently because, as is often the case with dreamwork, it would seem that all his inner work was slowly affecting his apparently intractable inner conflicts to the point of crisis and resolution. This was his dream:

I am in a city with a group of people, including my daughter. I am being pursued by a group of people. I flee by car down a freeway. The road becomes narrower as we leave the city: finally it becomes a bumpy track and I can drive no further. I continue on. I am now in bush country. I realise that my pursuers are occult practitioners who will submit me to dreadful and evil rituals I cannot refuse. I seem to be accompanied by an Aboriginal man.

We come to an old building that has a wide stairway going down to a basement. We go down with a lot of other people who are also Aborigines. They are white and dressed like city people, but I know from their eyes that they are Aboriginal. We come to a great hall that is lined with the bodies of dead people. This is the place where they are brought back to life. My Aboriginal companion says that such a person will then be redeemed.

Then I hear my pursuers outside. It/he/she comes in and is now a tiger. I know I have to fight it and am given a sword. As we fight, my weapons adapt to every twist and turn made by the tiger. I strike the tiger and it turns into a phallus made of paper. I unroll the phallus and read the message on it. It says, 'Strike me in Shiva and die.' I strike again with the sword.

The scene changes. Lights come on and I find I am the guest of honour at a ritual. My daughter and a young man ride in on white horses. It is a royal wedding and they are bride and groom. I wake with a deep sense of joy.

This dream is suggestive of profound transformation in a man hitherto at war with himself. It contains a great number of archetypal themes, and largely within an Australian context. First, there is the flight from the city (the site of most of his earlier struggles with the shadow) into the bush. As described earlier in chapter eleven, we have found, in a large number of

Australian people, that a journey into the bush or desert symbolises a descent into the deeper levels of the unconscious — the equivalent to a European's journey into the forest. This theme alone would suggest the possibility of renewal, discovery or transformation, possibly after confrontation with a witch, ogre or similar figure, as in all the best fairy tales.

As the dreamer journeys, he comes to be accompanied by an old Aboriginal — a wise guide. Note how, as in the last dream, the guide appears without fanfare and that he is not noticed again once he has imparted the information that he possesses. The destination is a magical cave where the 'dead' may be brought back to life and redeemed, in other words, where the dreamer will be able to renew and redeem his own inner life. Note that the dreamer had no Aboriginal friends or special knowledge of Aborigines. He was a 'middle Australian', but (like so many other Australians) he regarded Aboriginals as primitive but spiritual beings, who 'understood the country' (central Australia). Symbolically, in other words, the Aborigines were shadow-beings with knowledge of the inner unconscious, and, at least in this man's psyche, were guides to spiritual renewal.

The confrontation that then occurs is with an apparently sub-human and overwhelming destructive force. That is how it *feels* to the dreamer, of course. But, as is so often the case, the apparently overwhelming shadow figure is both easy to beat and connives in a positive outcome. The dreamer is provided with magical weapons, perhaps a result of all the inner work he had been doing, that easily defeat the tiger-phallus. The *latter* then instructs him perfectly clearly to strike it and die, that is, to undergo the symbolic death and resurrection necessary for renewal, and symbolised by so many things in the dream — from the underground vault, to the dead bodies that are brought to life there. The shadow figure both instructs him directly and, at the beginning of the dream, is perceived as 'intending to submit [him] to rituals [he] cannot refuse'. That, indeed, was the intention — but the rituals lead to renewal. It was only the ego's fear of the unconscious that made it perceive these rituals as 'dreadful and evil' at the beginning of the dream.

'Death and resurrection' are symbolised by a transformation of the whole scene and the beginning of a royal wedding. Reconciliation with the feminine side after a successful outcome of the struggle — or reconciliation — with the shadow, is occurring. It is very interesting, though, that the dream ego is not the bridegroom, but the guest of honour. This may have occurred because of the age of the dreamer. He is really now too old to identify completely with the archetype of the hero, as the royal bridegroom must. Rather, while the hero marries the bride in the dreamer's unconscious, ego consciousness is able to support the event, and be an important figure in it, but maintain a mature distance and independence from this overdue change.

The final point concerns the 'choice' of Shiva as the transformative god-figure. The dreamer was a Christian and denied any knowledge of Shiva — let alone that two of the latter's most common manifestations are as a tiger and a phallus (although one can never be sure that something one has casually heard or seen in childhood or later, has not been picked up by the unconscious for later use). What is interesting — if not surprising — is that the rather sterile, life-long Christianity of the dreamer could not be the conduit for inner renewal. It was too intertwined with unsuccessful habits and ego attitudes perhaps. One would hope, rather, that inner renewal might now itself become the conduit for a renewal of the dreamer's Christian understanding.

Notes

1. Leunig, M. 1990. *A Common Prayer*. Burwood, Vic.: HarperCollins (Collins Dove).
2. Guggenbuhl-Craig, A. 1982. *Power in the Helping Professions*. Zurich: Spring.

THE DREAM
Down I lay in a boat on the bay
and I dreamed about friends of the past
And while I was sleeping
The dream upward creeping
Had fastened itself to the mast

So blow all ye gales and fill up my sails
And carry me far, far away
Til my billowing dreams
All burst at the seams
As I lie in a boat on the bay

'The Dream' – Michael Leunig poem and illustration

14
DREAM INTERPRETATION

The longest journey is the journey within.

Dag Hammarskjold[1]

In this chapter you will find a series of guidelines, rules and resources for interpreting dreams that people have found helpful. These guidelines come in two parts, the first being step-by-step pointers relating to the dreamwork process, and the second a series of guiding principles to bear in mind when working with the insights that emerge.

Working with your Dreams

1. *Record your dream in a journal (see chapter fifteen)*

Read it through, comparing your written record with your memory of the experience. Note any additional parts you recall, any special observations, feelings and so on. Working in a group or with a partner may be helpful for some. Often another person can see things more clearly than we can, but it is important that we have the freedom to accept or reject those ideas as seems right to us. (See the following section on group work.)

2. *Ask — what does this mean to you?*

It is your dream, and only you know the meanings of it. Remember, dreams may have layers of meaning — there may not be simply one interpretation — and these may vary over time and place. (It can be quite revealing to return to a dream that occurred some time ago. New insights, associations and meanings may become evident that were unobserved the first time around.)

3. *Amplify the dream — through association*

Association is the process by which the symbolic meanings of the images in our dreams can be identified. An association is any image, feeling, sensation, word, idea etc. that comes to mind as we reflect on the symbol. For example, of a person in a dream, we might ask, 'Who is this person to me? What is he or she like? What incident or era does this person bring to mind?, What emotions, personality traits do I think of in relation to him or her?' The same approach would be taken for objects, for example, 'What do I think of when I see …' Recognise similar images, events and most particularly feelings; remember dream language is the language of the emotions.

Often a particular dream image may create a number of initial associations. Note them down, and try to resist the temptation to settle on only one too early in the process. Likewise, be wary of 'free associating' to an extent that detracts from the original dream. By this we mean coming up with one idea, and then creating an association to that idea, and so forth — a bit like playing a word game where one has to start a new word with the ending letter of the previous word!

In one dream, a person found himself playing a trumpet. Working with the dream, he was able to locate some of the focus of the dream chronologically (because he had learnt to play in primary school), but strong reactions also came with phrases such as 'blowing your own trumpet'. As a person who had struggled to accept his own abilities, and preferred to hide in the background, this became an especially significant symbol.

In another dream, he was required to touch an electric fence — the immediate association being that he was being invited to develop in areas that he felt were 'too shocking'.

4. *Are there any symbols that seem to have a universality to them?*

Some of the symbols that we encounter in dreams relate to the universal, what Jung called the 'collective unconscious'. These are memories, meanings and myths that are the common property of humanity. In previous chapters we have looked at some of the key archetypal symbols, but other more individual symbols abound. Water, for example, can often represent the unconscious, fire can be related to passion, or coins to hidden wisdom, ability, creativity. Birthing dreams often symbolise the arrival of a new insight, capacity or direction, while a lost birth may point us to some unresolved and unused dimension of ourselves. Lions, dragons, water, boats, magical rings, flying are just some of a myriad of such motifs and symbols that can appear.

In the following dream, we encounter not an archetype but a motif or symbol that has a powerful meaning and dimension to it. Occasionally, an event, or an animal interacting with the dream ego, reveals the ability for a new awareness or attitude before we are conscious of the change. This dream comes from a woman in her early thirties:

> *I dream that I meet a really big snake. It bites me on the back, and it is extremely painful. I woke up at this point and could still feel the pain of the bite, halfway down my back and on my right side.*

Over time, the woman had been working with her dreams, and had come to learn that the appearance of a snake for her nearly always signified some new insight or awareness about herself. The bigger the snake, perhaps, the more powerful was the insight.

Dealing still with the grief of her divorce, she came to an awareness on the day following the dream that she could have survived and developed as well as, or better than, she had, if she had not married. This was a discovery that she had been 'avoiding'. This, she saw, was the insight (painful and powerful), that the snake symbolised and brought to consciousness.

There are far too many sources to mention here, but a good knowledge of the collective wisdom, such as fairy tales, myths and legends etc. can be invaluable. References such as J. E. Cirlot's *A Dictionary of Symbols*[2] can also offer assistance, but it is important to look at these sources after one has done some initial reflection, not before. We are often tempted to be overly influenced by what the 'experts' say, rather than trusting our own insights. Above all, the question to ask is, 'Does the identification of such elements feel right to you?' If not, stick with your intuitive identifications, not those that others make. If they do help, then explore what the dream is saying about that dimension of your personality.

5. *Primarily all the symbols and people in dreams are elements of your self*

Each is symbolic, not real, in the sense that it is not your actual father, mother, lover etc. Learn the language of symbol, and resist the literal! (See the guidelines to follow.)

6. Emerging directions

Having assembled all these loose associations, can you see particular patterns or directions emerging? Are there events going on in life that the dream seems to be relating to? Explore the links, work intuitively, for what feels 'right'. For example, two women had very similar dreams of a dying child. One related this symbol to her ongoing grief for no longer being able to bear children. The other had been haunted by a series of these dreams, and came to understand them in the light of a part of herself that she had been neglecting. As she began to pay attention to this dimension of her life, she had a powerful dream of giving birth to this child. Our life context is critical in working with our dreams.

7. Is the dream part of a pattern?

Are there other dreams around this one that may be pointing in a similar direction? If we have been recording our dreams, it is not unusual to find the same themes cropping up over and over again, until we begin to address the issues they represent. We may also experience a series of dreams around a particular issue that we are working with, charting the inner progress we are making, and pointing us in the direction for the next step. Particular themes and patterns seem to occur at six- to twelve-month intervals.

8. Interaction with the dream may be very helpful

There are a number of ways of interacting with the dream. Some common methods include re-entering and dialoguing with the dream — a process called active imagination, which is described in more detail later in this chapter (for example, 'What would happen if I talked to the horse in my dream?'). Alternatively, passive Gestalt or acting out and imagining we are one of the objects in the dream, can be very helpful in enabling us to get in touch with some of the emotion and purpose of some of the symbols in a dream. But remember, we are not being *the living person*.

Drawing elements of the dream can also be a great way of working with a dream. One doesn't have to be a good artist — the process is what is important! (See the section later in this chapter.)

9. Begin to link the dream with the reality

What may be the message in the dream? Are there practical responses to be made? Use ritual to concretise the learning. (See the following section on ritual). Dreamwork is more than an interesting intellectual exercise. We are also invited to respond in action — 'What will I do/change/develop out of the insights of this experience?'

10. *Don't despair if things don't seem to come together*

Some dreams seem to fall into place, others require lots of work. Be gentle with yourself! Perhaps now is not the right time. Trust your own psyche that whatever needs to be worked through will emerge, one way or another, if you give yourself time, space and attention. Perhaps come back to it in a week's time and try again. Don't create pressure and make dreamwork a new goal or spiritual discipline that you must achieve!

Rules to Help in the Interpretation of Dreams

In chapters seven to thirteen, eleven rules for practical and safe dream analysis were noted at points in the text where they seemed most relevant. These may now be considered all together, in a little more detail and with some additional thoughts, both to remind you of the material we have covered and to make our approach to dream analysis as much of a cohesive whole as it can be. These rules have been put together from the recent, practical experience of the authors: they don't cover everything, but they do relate to the recent realities of practical dreamwork. Let's begin with the first three rules and the reasons why it is often advisable to seek skilled help when doing dreamwork.

Dream Analysis Rule One:

It is always easier to interpret another person's dreams than your own.

Dream Analysis Rule Two:

Be careful about attempting to deal with powerful dream material on your own: you can get overwhelmed. Remember that madness is freely available to everyone who gets too close to powerful, emotional and uncontrolled unconscious material.

Dream Analysis Rule Three:

Recurrent dreams of death or being overwhelmed, unrelieved by a later sense of renewal or growth, suggest that help with interpretation is needed.

Dreams, as we have seen in the earlier chapters, are consciously observed manifestations of the unconscious mind. And the human unconscious is probably the most complex structure in the known universe. It contains everything about us — instincts, emotions and thoughts that we don't yet know we have had, and spiritual experience. One of the most important reasons why this material is usually unconscious is simply that it is far too much for the conscious mind to perceive at any one time, let alone understand and/or assimilate. And we, as conscious ego personalities, are irretrievably enmeshed with it. Actually, we are a relatively insignificant part of the complexity of the mind — or so the unconscious often seems to 'think'!

It is therefore terribly difficult to understand one's own dreams. Every one of them is rooted in the same substratum from which consciousness gains its energies. We don't look at dreams, *we* are *a part of them*. The ego often gets caught up — even possessed — by the emotions of our own material and becomes unable to see beyond 'how it felt in the dream' (as so vividly illustrated by the 'monster' dream described in chapter seven). Objectivity is therefore very difficult to come by: most especially in relation to dream images that invoke our unconscious defence mechanisms. This is a major reason why one goes to a therapist, or even simply to a friend, to help us interpret our dreams. It is often easier for almost anyone else to understand our dreams. Their insights will be objective because they don't feel *with* the dream and they can save us an enormous amount of time and energy, sometimes to help break one's unconscious connectedness with dream images. Of course, by the same token, other people will also fail to perceive important aspects of our dreams that we haven't verbalised, but sometimes objectivity about the more obvious facets of a dream is what is most needed.

Help from another person — especially one experienced with dreamwork — can also be essential when we are bringing up a great deal of material or material that suggests we are in danger of being overwhelmed (which may be seen as being killed, swallowed up by a tidal wave, or otherwise disposed of in a dream). If the unconscious 'thinks' of consciousness as relatively important, the reverse is not the case. An example of this sort of thing was a client who dreamt at about weekly intervals that he was running along the road, chased by a lion. The lion always caught and killed him. After a few months of this dream, without seeking help, he experienced a major depressive episode that lasted nearly two years. The lion had eaten him, just as it had been threatening to do for so long. An experienced dream therapist will usually be able to pick up such signs of danger and help prevent the client being overwhelmed, by helping to deal with the negative material and by simply supporting the dreamer through the period of danger, or, sometimes, by closing down inner work until the dreamer has assimilated or ceased being troubled by this particular issue. And it should be noted that it is possible for anyone to bring up too much unconscious material, and be in danger of being overwhelmed. Even the strongest ego can become weak and defenceless when confronted by major inner conflicts, let alone by images of important archetypal material, or even the divine.

The next rule is concerned with the sort of dream experiences that suggest when therapy, or at least analysis of a particular problem, is indicated.

Dream Analysis Rule Four:

If unconscious material appears in dreams as multiple figures, or in recurrent dreams that wake the dreamer, analysis and understanding is often indicated.

The basis of this rule is the frequent finding that when an unconscious conflict has a great deal of, or is gaining in, energy, it seems to force itself to your attention. Being repeatedly awoken from sleep is such a situation, as is to repeatedly waken in a distressed state, or to have dreams of terrible or overwhelming situations when one is *not* already in dream analysis. (Dream analysis, of course, also often tends to provoke confrontations with strong unconscious material). Less threatening, but also suggesting that further exploration might be productive, are dreams of multiple figures (for example, a known person who appears in triplicate in a dream), or dreams where the dreamer experiences — and perhaps enjoys — events or emotions from which she or he would recoil in waking life.

The next two of the rules for analysis are reminders of the wonder and extent of the material experienced in dreams.

Dream Analysis Rule Five:

Everything that you see in a dream is a property of your own mind — your own unconscious beauty, power or emotions — as observed, but not owned, by the ego.

Dream Analysis Rule Six:

In crisis periods, almost every major archetypal theme may by present in one's dream life. A positive outcome may be hoped for if themes of spiritual experience or renewal begin to appear in dreams.

It can be very difficult to persuade to people to acknowledge and own the enormous creativity and beauty of their unconscious mind. Quite often therapists need to tell clients with some firmness that the beautiful maiden, or handsome prince, or powerful panther, or holy music that they have just seen or heard, is a part of *them*. Psychologically unwounded people — for example, many people in tribal societies — do not need to be reminded of this. They are aware of their own beauty, holiness and inner importance. It is a sad reflection on our society that we are not. As Robert Johnson points out in *Owning Your Own Shadow*[3], people are often quite willing to acknowledge their inner, unconscious evil or ugliness, but will run a mile rather than acknowledge their inner beauty and strength — *that* would mean owning, and living up to, God's demand that we become all that is in us to become!

Rule six also makes the point that some of the most beautiful and complex experiences are induced by periods of crisis and change. Of course, at the time they may seem far more anxiety-provoking or terrifying and threatening than beautiful, but afterwards the person who has been through the fire will be able to acknowledge the depth and spiritual value of his or her experience.

The final five rules have in common the need to test dream experiences against objective reality whenever possible.

Dream Analysis Rule Seven:

When you meet an image (for example, a shadow element) in a dream that seems hostile (or has other negative characteristics) always check out what it actually did or said. Distinguish your subjective impressions from the objective events of the dream.

This rule makes the particular point that our experiences of figures and events in our dreams are often contaminated by our ego-attitudes — that the apparent hostility, or evil, or indeed beauty of a dream figure is as likely to be a projection of an ego-attitude as a real characteristic of the figure itself. If you see something in a dream that seems hateful, in other words, this may merely tell you that you *think* of it as hateful, it doesn't actually tell you what it is *really* like! Actions tell the story. If a dream object seems detestable, but does nothing to justify that attitude on the part of the ego, then you are probably being fooled by your own attitude (as in the 'New York' dream example in the last chapter).

Dream Analysis Rule Eight:

Doing something (for example, having sex) in a dream is not the same as doing it in the everyday world.

Dream Analysis Rule Nine:

Don't act out your dreams with real people. Always remember that the 'people' in dreams are parts of you and not those people in the everyday world that they may happen to resemble.

These rules make the point that the dream world and the everyday world are always separate. Of course, events seen in a dream may represent wish-fulfilment or, if you prefer, are contaminated by everyday thoughts and wishes. But even then they are nearer to fantasy than acting out, and always have additional, symbolic meaning. And, importantly, they do not affect others, unless we make it so!

Following on from this, you should make sure that they *stay* separate. Your dreams are internal events, following the rules of the unconscious. They should be taken seriously and dealt with seriously on that understanding.

Rule Nine also makes an important point about acting out. When you 'see' someone you know in a dream, it means that you have 'put their face' on an internal psychic image because there must be some degree of correspondence between your perception of the other person and your own internal material that you have picked up. Then, when you 'see' the person in your dream, you become internally aware of the resemblance (consciously or unconsciously). Having done this, it becomes much easier for you to re-project your internal material onto the real-life individual. You then feel connected to the latter, often in a much stronger way. The danger here is that you may now begin to act and feel towards them in a different way, perhaps even to act as though you 'own' them (as you do your internal images). They are very likely to sense the difference and feel uncomfortable or resentful: no one likes being suddenly treated in a different manner by a friend or relative when there has been no overt cause for the change.

All this said, though, it should be admitted that sometimes trying to find out why one has introjected a particular person's image (if it can be done without affecting the latter) can help people to understand the workings of their psyche. A recent example of this was a client in analysis who had periodically, for over five years, dreamed that his wife had left him: he was invariably passive, helpless and grief-stricken in these dreams. The wife denied any such real-life intentions. Over the next two or three years he did a great deal of work with these dreams, on the assumption that they related to the relationship between his mother/anima images (which the 'wife' was assumed to represent) and his ego. He became progressively less helpless and became able to confront the internal 'wife' or to let her go her way with equanimity. A more creative, gentle and nurturing personality began to develop. At this point the wife, without warning, actually did leave him! She claimed to have developed this intention only over the last two or three years. In this particular case there was no doubt, upon analysis, that the husband had unconsciously perceived a latent intention (also unconscious) in the wife and that this intention corresponded in some way to his image of his own internal feminine. This may even have been an important reason for the marriage in the first place. The wife's actions, in turn, may have been precipitated (or liberated) by the diminishment of the husband's unconscious helplessness of attitude, and so on. In a case like this it is never fully possible to disentangle the complex interactions of intra-psychic and real-life events. We can only be sure that the husband's inner work made the break, when it came, more easy to bear.

Dream Analysis Rule Ten:

Don't try to resolve your remaining parental complexes by re-projecting them onto a surviving real-life parent. If you are over thirty years old, they are yours now, and no one else's!

Even when another person (most often a parent or other near relative) may have been instrumental in giving you a complex or conflict, once you have it, it is yours and yours alone. It is very bad policy *ever* to project your problems onto others and try to drag them into your inner world. It is both unfair and counter-productive.

Dream Analysis Rule Eleven:

Erotic dreams about parent figures, or other persons who are not legitimate sexual partners, should always be checked out in relation to real-life events, but are usually symbolic of the need for love or intimacy and often have an erotic nature because this is the only means of expression of love for many people.

This final rule has become increasingly important in a society where some therapists habitually attempt to uncover repressed memories of sexual abuse. This attitude is, in some ways, a natural reaction to a long period where sexual abuse of children was often overlooked or denied. But it can lead to the equally terrible result of destroying parent–child relationships and family life without reason. So, always check out dreams of sexual relations with parents or others with whom such relations would not be permissible, remembering the possibility of later unconscious sexualisation of earlier loving but non-abusive interactions.

Using Active Imagination in Dreamwork

Active imagination is a term to describe using our imagination as a means of exploring unconscious material. It is basically a technique of consciously dialoguing — talking and listening — with the different dimensions of one's unconscious self.

Active imagination is a discipline in its own right. Jung suggested it is an even more important way of encountering the unconscious than dreams, because it offers the opportunity for the conscious and unconscious to interact on neutral ground — in the arena of our imagination — and to work together. It is also a useful technique for exploring dreams, as it gives us the chance to expand, and delve into, the symbols in a dream that may be unclear.

Evidently, the use of active imagination may actually cause dreaming to decrease, perhaps because it provides an alternative avenue for unconscious material to be presented to us. But it is also worth noting that it is a powerful technique, and one to be used wisely and respectfully. It is important to have someone who is experienced whom we can contact if we feel we are being overwhelmed by the encounter. (This is indeed true of all dreamwork.)

In its simplest form, active imagination involves imagining a scenario from a dream, and re-exploring it, in order to extend and expand it. If we have made use of religious led meditations, such as those by Francis Loyola, we will be on familiar ground. But whereas a led meditation has a degree of direction and focus, sometimes even a pre-meditated outcome, active imagination is far more open-ended and unstructured.

Robert Johnson[4] suggests a four-step approach to using our imagination, after some initial background preparation. Preparation includes readiness to record, preferably in written form, our imaginary encounter, a little like writing a conversation. It is an activity that is either done alone (with the provisos mentioned above) or in the company of someone who is trusted implicitly. Because we are unfamiliar with such activities, we may easily find ourselves feeling embarrassed, or seek to 'perform' for others. We need to be able to express ourselves in both active and passive ways without feeling as if we are being watched or judged.

The first step is called *invitation*. Here we invite the characters and scenario of the dream to fill our minds. We might pick out one particular character that we are uncertain about, imagine it, and prepare to ask it some questions. Feeling relaxed enough to do so may take time and practice. It is better to go easily and travel at our own 'comfort level'.

An additional suggestion, that may act as both an aid to getting started and as a precaution to getting 'lost', is to imagine an object through which the imagination exercise is begun and ended. For example, we might imagine that we put on a particular item of clothing (perhaps a jacket or special shoes) or alternatively that we have a special word that takes us to the 'dream world' and, upon its repetition, always brings us back to everyday reality.

The second stage is *dialogue*. This is where we might ask questions of the character or characters (whether human, animal, or inanimate), and 'listen' to the responses that seem to be made. We might also simply 'sit with' the character, gaining a sense of its purpose and feeling. We might check out our original feelings about it. For example, if we were afraid of it, we might approach it and see its response. Extended conversations can even be held: arguments, discussions — all sorts of things. There is a fine line, however, that is only learnt through experience, between encouraging dialogue, and forcing, or controlling the actions and responses of the characters in our imagination exercise.

Adding an ethical element of values, as a third stage, can be a little difficult to comprehend, and is open to debate. The basis of the idea is that the ego-consciousness must set limits on the exercise, in order to be profitable and not de-humanising and destructive. As we become aware of unconscious attitudes and dimensions of our selves, we will need to decide what we are to do with these insights. This involves choices of an ethical nature[5]. Johnson tells of an example Jung used to explain this point. A young man dreamed that his girlfriend slid into an icy lake and was drowning. Jung advised the man to use active imagination, and go and rescue her, get her dry clothes, and care for her — exactly as he would in real life. 'It is as much the ego's duty to bring this sense of responsibility to the creations of the inner world as it is for us to tend to the welfare of our fellow humans.'[6]

When using active imagination, Johnson writes:

First, you add the ethical element by holding out for the attitudes and conduct that are consistent with your character and deepest values.

Second, ethical balance requires that we not let one archetype or one part of ourselves take over at the expense of the others. We can't sacrifice essential values in order to pursue one narrow urge or goal.

Third, we must nurture and preserve the specifically human values that serve human life, that keep practical daily life going, and that keep our human relationships alive.[7]

However, this approach is not without controversy. Many other therapists would argue that it is in active imagination that we have the opportunity to name and bring to the surface, and then deal with, many emotions, feelings and attitudes that have been suppressed — that we are ashamed of, or find unacceptable — in real life. Active imagination may create an environment (with boundaries) where we may express anger, for example, so that the energy can be diffused, and not brought into the outer world. Alternatively it may suppress and bottle things up to cause problems later on.

The danger with the former possibility is that it can potentially subvert the healing process, because uncomfortable issues and attitudes can be avoided in the name of ethical choice. For example, in the example of the drowning woman, one obvious question that is not asked is: Why is (he) the dreamer, letting/wanting to see this part of his psyche 'drown'? She may well need to be 'rescued', and valued, but that is further down the track. Seeking to 'behave ethically' at this point begins to treat the dream imagery as something more than symbolic.

Clearly, we are required to live as, and be, ethical people. However, it may be that our ethical choices are those that emerge when we are most aware of the full range of our weaknesses and strengths. Johnson's ethical approach (above) is perhaps more applicable as we move out of active imagination and into everyday life.

The fourth step, *making it concrete with physical ritual*, is an important part of dreamwork, and is covered in more detail below.

To summarise then, active imagination is an extremely helpful technique, used respectfully, to gain fresh insight into our dreams, particularly when their meaning or purpose seems unclear.

Drawing

In the section below, we will be talking about the importance of ritual as a physical act. Drawing, too, as a physical activity, can be especially useful when working with dreams. This may involve drawing the whole dream or a particular symbol or event. The process may help us to comprehend the meaning of a symbol and to discover which part of it seems to have the most connection for us. For example, one person was working with an image that had appeared in a dream of a hand gently supporting a breast. After working with the image through drawing, he made the discovery that his connection was very much with the hand and the supportive energy it symbolised. There was nothing sexual about the image — it described for him his own role and ability both as one who was able to support, but who also needed to be supported.

Likewise, another confusing dream contained a rainbow with little colour in it. When it was drawn, certain colours 'leapt' out for the drawer, for whom, by exploring associations with the colours, the meaning of the dream became clear.

The thought of drawing can be quite intimidating to those of us who have little in common with the Da Vincis and Rembrandts of this world, but technical ability is not important! Rather, it is the activity itself that seems to be most therapeutic, and the simplest of drawings can start the discovery process flowing. In fact, if we are good technical drawers, we can sometimes get distracted with the practicalities of the exercise, rather than letting drawing be an emotional event that is inviting some of our unused dimensions to have a voice. Crayons are especially good, because it is easy (without the hassle of oils) to convey texture as well as image.

The Use of Ritual

> *Any object or event is sacramental in which the transcendent is perceived to be present. Sacramental objects are holy objects, laden with divine power. Paul Tillich*[9]

When we talk of ritual, what exactly do we mean? One helpful definition is: 'a symbolic behaviour, consciously performed.'[10] Unfortunately, as we have seen, much of the language of symbol and myth has been lost to our culture, and consequently so has much of our familiarity with ritual. Our immediate associations with the word itself may be quite negative — ritual as repetitious, irrelevant, something that happens in cathedrals etc.

And yet, our life is already constructed of hundreds of tiny patterns of action, or rituals, helpful and unhelpful, that create some sense of purpose or meaning for our lives. We might always fold our clothes in a particular way or have a special little pattern of actions we go through before filling out the lotto coupon! Such rituals often serve the purpose of creating a sense of security and stability for us. But rituals can equally help us to own and develop patterns of change. Rituals may involve lots of people and be major events and spectacles, or they may be solitary observances and very simple concrete actions. It will be our connection with them that creates the significance, and in the identification with a ritual, especially if we have created it ourselves, enormous energy and power for transformation can be released. Those who are actively involved in a religious tradition will be well aware of this. Celebration of the Eucharist, passing the peace, rites of baptism and many other worship experiences are corporate rituals that, when we connect ourselves to them, assist in the potential for transformation and change.

'Earthing out' or physicalising the learning gained from dreams is extremely important. Too often an insight gained from a dream can remain nothing more than that. The actual application, both for our inner world and for our interaction in the wider community, remains undeveloped. Carrying out some sort of physical act or representation helps to affirm the underlying message of the dream, and moves us from an abstract, and at times intellectual understanding, into the world of concrete reality. Such 'earthing out' might be as mundane as committing ourselves to some personal space and time each day, to further contemplate our lives, or involve a profound change in the way we undertake a particular activity. One person, after a series of dreams involving 'sailing on the waters of the unconscious', took up sailing a small dinghy as one way in which the journey within could be affirmed.

We need to exercise some care to ensure that the ritual, or concretising activity, is appropriate, and continues to point us to the work to be done, and does not subvert us from the dream imagery itself. Likewise, 'earthing out' learning is not the same as 'acting out' our dreams. In reference to the anima and animus, for example, the dangers of enacting dream behaviour inappropriately was underlined. The same is true of ritual. Be aware that we are to 'earth out' our insights, and not 'act out' our images.[11]

If we are part of a religious community, we have at our disposal a great wealth of ritual, liturgy, prayer, music, drama, dance and worship which, with a little creativity, can be the basis for profound expressions of the naming of our learning.

Many of the great rituals of the church can easily become resources for celebrating and affirming our growth and discoveries. For example, the rite of confession, in its fullest sense, is the owning not just of our shortcomings, failure or sin, but is also an affirmation of our strengths, steps and discoveries towards growth and healing. With this understanding, liturgies of confession take on a powerful new meaning. Likewise, the central sacrament of the Eucharist, which underpins our common life, is a ritual that can be creatively presented and experienced as an 'ownership' liturgy.

In addition to participating in the regular worship life of a congregation, working as a small group, a number of people with a common interest in dreamwork and spiritual development can easily develop a series of liturgies that speak directly to the life experience and learning of the group members. Use your imagination! Candles, simple prayers, drawings, music and dance can all be incorporated to form powerful symbolic representations of our lives and faith journeys. Creating opportunities where people can tell of their stories and self-discoveries, naming the joys and sorrows of life, and seeking to relate that to their spiritual journeys, is a powerful and healing gift to be able to offer one another.

It is important to recall the earlier definition we used for ritual. Ritual is physical. While words can play an significant part in ritual, it is the action, and the involvement where possible of the whole body, and of all of the senses, that is of paramount importance. By ritualising something, we are trying to allow the insight to move beyond our mind, to permeate our whole being. If such ideas seem strange or uncomfortable, we might want to state clearly the link or representation that we wish to express, to help ourselves become familiar with the language and symbolism for ritual. For example, we might use a rock, and place it on a table, saying, 'This rock is the part of myself that is ...', having felt its weight and texture with our hands, its coldness on our cheek, its smell etc. If the rock was used as a symbol of an obstacle or issue we had to overcome, we might even develop a ritual where the rock was smashed with a hammer, or was rearranged in some manner, symbolising a change in form, substance and energy.

A helpful place to start, if you are feeling hesitant, may be to use some prepared liturgies and adapt them to your own situation. One excellent book that springs to mind is *More than Words: Prayer and Ritual for Inclusive Communities*, by Janet Schaffran and Pat Kozak (Crossroad 1992). It contains a wide range of prayers and liturgies for a variety of life events, as well as lists of useful symbols, and guidelines for creating your own liturgies and reflections on inclusive language.

In our appendix, you will also find two simple liturgies for use with dreamwork.

In conclusion, it is important to remember that the church has a long tradition of offering spiritual direction. More and more people are interested in finding a spiritual director or mentor, in both Catholic and Protestant traditions. The importance of spiritual direction is being rediscovered as foundational for theological education, and its importance for all people is being affirmed. Depending on your own faith community and geographic location, developing a relationship with someone appropriately trained in direction, and with a degree of familiarity and expertise with dreamwork, may not be easy, but is certainly worth the effort. Just as there is a growing recognition for the need for interdisciplinary studies in secular education, the creative melding of Jungian psychological insight and the tradition of spiritual direction provide a powerful resource for spiritual, personal and community growth.

Group Work

Working in a small group with others interested in dream analysis can be an encouraging and inspiring activity. Because of the intimate nature of our dreams, groups that work best tend to be small (three to six members), and for some people, even a group is a little threatening, and they would prefer to work with a guide or on their own. It is important to find the structure that suits you best.

What then, are the major benefits of working in a group?

- A group provides discipline. Dreamwork can be emotionally draining. Belonging to a group can provide an incentive to keep on with the work of recording and reflecting on dreams.

- Groups provide a 'safe' framework in which to do dreamwork. Some of the dangers we may encounter have been mentioned elsewhere. A group may assist in preventing us from being overwhelmed and help us when we feel vulnerable.
- There is a strange paradox in dreamwork that while only we carry the real meaning of the dream, others may often see it before we do. Others in a group can challenge our own biases and encourage us to check out a breadth of meanings. The temptation when working in isolation is to consciously or unconsciously avoid issues that are challenging. A group 'keeps us honest'!
- One of the major functions of a group is the offering of encouragement and support. It is comforting to know that others are with us in our joys and struggles and may be thinking and praying for us even when the group is not together.
- A small group is a natural environment for ritual making and enacting. In a group setting, liturgies, poems, dance, drama etc. can be used as powerful means of concretising our learning (see below).

In order to gain these sorts of benefits, some groundwork and agreement needs to be reached by group members:

- It is important that the group contains some members who have knowledge of dreamwork principles, and that all members are prepared to continue learning together. Simply sharing common ignorance may not be all that helpful! (Attending some introductory courses may be a good way to gain some basic preparation, and may also provide the opportunity to meet others with common interests.)
- Members need to make a group covenant based on their trust of each other. There must be just as much freedom not to share as to share.
- Confidentiality is critical. In sharing our dreams, we are sharing part of ourselves. It is important that what is offered in the security of the group is treated with respect and confidentiality.
- A group will need to clarify some boundaries of competence. What are the sorts of issues that people feel they have the experience to work with, and what are those that are beyond the collective ability of the group? If particular issues emerge, the group might seek outside assistance or encourage the person concerned to seek such help.

Additional Guidelines for Spiritual Development and Dreamwork

For those engaged in dreamwork who also have a Christian or religious perspective, some further suggestions about dream interpretation may be helpful.

First, it is important to remember, as we have mentioned elsewhere, that our personal and spiritual growth are interwoven within the psyche. We are also connected to others on an interpersonal level, and with our role and place within the life of our religious and social community. We are seeking to understand ourselves, our place in the scheme of things and to develop a growing awareness of, and relationship with, God.

As Leroy Howe, a professor of theology and pastoral care, writes:

Self-development, therefore, is to be seen in the light of such calling as aiming toward a life of serving God in all things. Spiritual guidance provides support, encouragement, insight, and if necessary, confrontation, to enable persons to come to terms with their own respective callings to service. Since one way in which God's call is issued is through dreams, the fundamental question to be asked of any and all dreams is whether there is yield in them for discerning the calling of a particular person or a particular group to new kinds of service in God's name.[11]

Second, the guidelines presented earlier in this chapter are an indispensable framework for dream interpretation, whatever our religious persuasion. But for those who are part of a faith community, special attention can be given to some of the specific resources at their disposal.

As we have seen, a knowledge and understanding of the mythology, traditions and symbols of our culture, both past and present, are essential in understanding archetypes. For those steeped in the Christian tradition, a familiarity with the symbols, stories and mythology of the Scriptures, an understanding of the church and its strengths and weaknesses, and thoughtful reflection upon one's own life and experience of faith in the world, provide additional resources for personal work. Therefore, in commencing dreamwork, if we are not familiar with the tradition that has shaped us, and formed a significant part of the universal collective unconscious, then some reading and development in these areas will prove invaluable. Our framework of faith and belief will serve as a useful background and aid in helping us to discern the meaning of dreams.

Third, dreams that we have made the effort to record are likely to prove more useful than our working with an *ad hoc* approach. This is the case for all dreamwork, regardless of our philosophical framework. Our religious tradition reinforces this point with a long history of recognising that for our soul to be nurtured a certain amount of spiritual discipline is required. Further suggestions for recording and remembering dreams can be found in chapter fifteen.

Fourth, our life context is important to understanding our dreams. Dreams are located in a place and time, and we should not forget to examine our understanding of what is going on in our lives at the time — what issues, concerns, orientations are playing upon us. To this can be added a further question: *'What is our understanding of ourselves, as a person of faith, and what are the faith issues that are 'alive' for us, at this point in time?'*

In this way, we can locate our personal growth in the framework of our faith, and see our personal growth and self-understanding linked to our relationship with God and our faith community. In addition, our own 'inner' growth may then challenge and stretch our faith understanding, and the faith tradition can in turn provoke us to consider more deeply the connection between self, God and the Christian community.

A final point for reflection is one that returns us to where we began, and that is the question of *purpose and direction*. In common with a Jungian perspective, the Christian community is one that is to be oriented towards growth and development, individually and corporately (it is tragic that the history of our tradition is full of situations of denial and limitation, but the higher ideal remains). In approaching dreams, therefore, we move with cautious optimism that the unconscious material we encounter is being presented for the purpose of growth towards individuation, as Jung called it, or what may be seen as represented by terms such as wholeness, sanctity, etc. in religious language. Dreams may be a means by which we gain not only new insight into ourselves, but into our relationship with God.

In committing ourselves to dreamwork, we will need to be open to the presence of God as the source of that growth. Such work involves the shattering, often painfully, of immature faith and theology, as well as self-understanding. When we feel overwhelmed, or threatened by such growth, it may be helpful to remember that, in being Christian, we are followers of the crucified One — the One who did not avoid the pain of life, but embraced it, and travelled through it. Our faith in this way is not to be one that provides us with a crutch or fortress against the pain and struggle of life, or promises an easier life, but rather is the infusion of God, and the hope and promise of God's presence, into our very living and growing.

Wholeness is the emergence of a restfulness within a life of paradox. It is not a state where all negative things are absent, but where good and bad, tragedy and comedy, sadness and joy, pain and ecstasy are seen as the gifts of soul-making and of nurturing the divine spirit within us.

Your Dream Therapist or Guide

While many people may discover helpful supportive relationships and guidance through spiritual direction, reputable courses or a group, there often comes a time when a greater level of expertise is essential.

As you have seen in this book, dream analysis is a time-consuming, difficult and occasionally dangerous task that requires dedication and honesty and, often, skilled help. For this reason, it is often advisable to work with a trained psychotherapist or equivalent helper.

However, if you do seek such help, it really must be expert! And there are, unfortunately, many people working in this area who are not expert at all: some can be more of a danger than a help. Some are simply inexperienced, others, while genuinely interested in dreamwork, have not yet dealt well enough with their own material to be able to help others.

Some are motivated to work in the area by their own unconscious (shadow) problems and may project these or the therapeutic relationship, onto you, so that you become an unwilling part of someone else's neurosis! Some have qualifications in areas (for example, psychology, theology or medicine) that they consider entitle them to work in an area that, in reality, they may know nothing about and yet others are simply trying to make a quick buck by offering rapid and simplistic explanations and 'fixes'.

Unfortunately, many 'new age' therapists fall into some or all of the above categories. So, if you are seeking professional help with your dreamwork, you do need to ask, and get, clear answers to a number of important questions.

First, and most obviously, the understanding of dreams should be a major area of interest — and experience — for the therapist. Don't work with anyone who says things like, 'Well, dreams aren't really my area, but

I don't mind having a go.' Your friends won't know much about dreams either, but at least they won't charge you money! The therapist should also have done a lot of work with his or her own dream material — for example, by having undergone Jungian or Freudian analysis. Ask — you have the right to know and an experienced therapist will be happy to tell you. If the therapist is experienced in dreamwork you should also check his or her orientation (or 'school'). You might, for example, be happy to work with a Freudian therapist if your dreams indicate problems with sexuality: perhaps not in other cases.

If there is a claim of adherence to a school you have never heard of, ask what the theory of the meaning of dreams is for that school. If you can't understand the answer you probably shouldn't go any further. Dream analysis requires clear thought, and the clear language that goes with it. This brings up the ancillary point that, other things being equal, you should always work with a therapist whose language (and hopefully value system) most resembles your own — for ease and clarity of communication.

If the opportunity arises, you should talk to several therapists about the possibility of working with them. You will need to be comfortable with, and on a similar wavelength to, your therapist if he or she is going to help you; go with your gut feeling. If this initial talk is conducted like a clinical interview, or the therapist charges you a fee for it, put that person back at the end of the queue!

On the subject of money, don't be shy to ask about fees in detail. A relatively simple problem, involving perhaps a recurrent dream, can be fairly easily accounted for, but serious dreamwork is more usually a long-term undertaking (anything from twenty to three hundred hours) and can be very expensive. Most good psychotherapists will minimise their fees to enable you to do the amount of work you need, so negotiate.

It is very important not to start work, become involved in a positive and therapeutic experience of real value, and then have to stop in the middle because you run out of money. Your unconscious mind will be very unhappy about it indeed! While checking out the money side, try to make sure that the therapist is willing to undertake long-term work, and to work with you periodically, as needed. It is a common finding in dreamwork that material comes up (say, a confrontation with the shadow) that needs to be dealt with over twenty or thirty sessions.

After this, there is a pause — a period of inner peacefulness — while the outcome of the work is assimilated. Then, maybe six months later, the next stage appears (let's say a confrontation with the anima/animus) and more dreamwork is required. This is a perfectly normal way of doing inner business, but may not suit the orderly minds of some therapists.

A word on qualifications. A *psychiatrist* is a medical doctor who specialises in illnesses involving the mind. He or she will be expert at the diagnosis of mental illnesses and the physical treatments of these, but may or may not be qualified in psychotherapy. Most, in fact, will not undertake long-term, close personal psychotherapy. Those that do, and are good at it, are in great demand, as they can come free (if they bulk bill).

A *registered psychologist* has at least an honours degree in psychology and either postgraduate qualifications or two years' practical experience. Like the psychiatrist, the psychologist may, or may not, have experience of psychotherapy and the meaning of dreams. You need to check out their experience in this area, as outlined above, along with their orientation. Many psychologists, often those with a behavioural, research or cognitive orientation, discount the worth of dreamwork. Some are even quite hostile to the value of such work and the ideas of the Jungians!

An *analyst* is a person who has undergone training as a psychotherapist at an appropriate institute. A psychoanalyst will have undergone Freudian training; a Jungian analyst will have been trained at a Jung Institute (of which there are a couple of dozen throughout the world). An analyst will have undergone a prolonged personal analysis and should have the appropriate institute's diploma. He or she *should* be relatively expert at therapy although, disappointingly, it has been our experience that this is not always the case. Some analysts are — to be courteous — exceedingly eccentric, while others have problems relating to the external world as it is today. So, even with a fully trained analyst, be very careful about whether he or she is the person for *you*.

Finally, the title *psychotherapist* has no legal meaning at present. Anyone can call themselves a psychotherapist and stick up a sign. This is not to say that some psychotherapists who are neither psychiatrists nor psychologists are not good. Some of them are among the best psychotherapists around: many of these are from other areas of the helping professions, have done their own psychotherapeutic work and are using their experience to work as psychotherapists rather than trying to gain academic qualifications. But you should always check out their knowledge and areas of interest (again, as described above) before working with them.

Notes

1. Harcourt, G. 1985. *Dawn Through our Darkness: Prayers and Reflections*. London: Collins. p. 164.
2. Cirlot, J. E. 1995. *A Dictionary of Symbols*. London: Routledge.
3. Johnson, R. 1991. *Owning Your Own Shadow: Understanding the Dark Side of the Psyche*. New York: HarperCollins.
4. Johnson, R. 1986. *Inner work: using dreams and active imagination for personal growth*. San Francisco: Harper & Row.
5. Price, S. & Thompson, D. 1993. *Think!* Melbourne: JBCE. The Christian tradition, and faith, can be helpful in this regard, if we use it as a dynamic resource to shape the process of our thinking, rather than as a set of beliefs or commandments to be followed without question. Steve Price and David Thompson offer further discussion and practical guidelines on this topic.
6. Johnson, R. 1986. *Inner Work: Using Dreams and Active Imagination for Personal Growth*. San Francisco: Harper & Row. p. 190.
7. Johnson, R. ibid, p. 192.
8. Martos, J. 1981. *Doors to the Sacred*. London: SCM. p. 9.
9. Johnson, R. ibid, p. 102.
10. 'Acting out' events etc. is an important part of therapy. However, it is a process done within the boundaries of a therapeutic experience — it is not necessarily the public ritualising of our fantasies and imaginings.
11. Howe, L. 1986. Dream interpretation in spiritual guidance. *Journal of Pastoral Care*, 40, September, p. 264.

Dawn over the pondage, Lake Eildon, Victoria. (*Photograph by Steve Price.*)

REMEMBERING DREAMS

'After that,' continued the Hatter, 'I cut some more bread and butter —'
'But what did the Dormouse say?' one of the jury asked.
'That I can't remember,' said the Hatter.
*'You **must** remember,' remarked the King, 'or I'll have you executed.'*

(Alice in Wonderland)[1]

For some people, each night is filled with dreams. They wake up in the morning and can recall quite clearly the adventures of the night before. Their problem is in deciding which dreams to work with! For others, dreams seem to come rarely, and are often fleeting images at best.

Can we improve the recall of our dreams? A few practical guidelines can actually help. It is a quite common occurrence that once we make a decision to do some dreamwork, we begin to remember our dreams. And, as Jung was quick to point out, these early dreams (in the course of his sessions with patients) were particularly important in revealing the areas in which it would be most beneficial for us to work.

Each of the following ideas can work for you. However, it is important to approach the subject in a fairly relaxed manner. These ideas are not a set of rules or a new pattern that must be followed slavishly. Rather, they are a collection of hints that others have found helpful. Find which ones work best for you, and be ready to add your own!

1. Use a Notebook or Dream Journal

Go out and buy a special book in which you intend to record your dreams and your notes about them. While a normal exercise book may do, purchasing something a little special may help the project take on extra importance and significance. Dreams are a special part of you. Cherish them, and treat them with respect, and they will prove to be valuable. Some people who are artistically inclined like to illustrate the book as well — and it becomes a special testimony to the spiritual journey they have undertaken.

While writing some notes on scraps of paper next to the bedside table may be the best solution at three o'clock in the morning, transferring them into your journal not only makes sure they do not go through the washing machine, but also gives them a more tangible presence as part of yourself.

The idea of writing up a dream may appear daunting at first, but you will quickly be amazed at how it assists recall. Struggling with the words seems to give space for the dream to become focussed, and our early memories of the dream are recorded. Our memory a few days later may have changed, but if the dream has been recorded we will have a more accurate snapshot both of the dream, and of its associated emotions.

2. Make the Effort!

Depending on how often you dream, you may not find it possible to record all your dreams. That could become a full-time occupation! However, creating the discipline of regularly writing up your dreams does assist recall. Sometimes you may get a sense that a dream is especially important or significant. Try and record such ones as soon as possible. It is remarkable how quickly even significant dreams turn into vague recollections and are forgotten if we do not make an effort to pay conscious attention to them.

3. Aiding Recall

Before beginning to write down a dream, lie down or sit quietly with your eyes closed, and go through the dream from start to finish at least once. This aids in 'switching on' your short-term memory and will assist you in remembering the sequence of the dream and some of the details that will emerge as being significant.

A good time to remember dreams is when you have just awakened. Keep your journal by your bedside, and if you have time in the middle of the morning rush, create some space to write up the dream. Often by the time we have got up, dressed, read the paper, eaten the Cornflakes, and a myriad of other distractions have occurred, we may find that our dream has already slipped away back into the unconscious.

4. Don't Alter Your Dream!

As you begin to write or retell a dream, you may discover that you are subtly altering the sequence and story of the dream to make it more sensible and logical! Seek to record dreams in all their 'nonsense', avoiding the temptation to interpret as you write. Often dream material seems strange or outlandish. Sequences may appear to be back to front, or have no logical order or chronology. Sometimes dream imagery will be embarrassing, yet by preserving it as best you can in its 'native' form, sense will be made of the dream in time. Don't assume that some part of the dream is unimportant or insignificant — often the parts we are tempted to overlook reveal the greatest truths!

If we compare our early recording of the dream with how it is remembered a few days later, significant differences may appear. These differences can often provide a great resource for insight and understanding. A good way of seeing this is to get a friend to have your written version of the dream in front of them while you tell them the dream verbally. They will quickly be able to identify the changes that have occurred, either in reconstruction or omission.

5. What Do I Write?

Try to record as much detail as you can. With long and complex dreams, this can become quite a task, but don't become disheartened. In time, you will begin to learn just how to write up a dream in a fashion that is most helpful to you. Seek to record not only the obvious, but the strange and insignificant things that you recall. Colours, shapes, ages of people, what they were wearing etc. can all be important clues and symbols for unravelling the dream.

6. I Can't Remember ...

If you don't remember very much of a dream, try to record what you do remember. A few fleeting images may be enough to open up the dream's meaning further down the track, particularly when the dream is part of a series.

Sometimes we may wake up with an absolute certainty that we have had an important dream, but can remember nothing at all. When this happens, don't despair. Rather, trust yourself, and God, that the issue will be presented again, perhaps in another way. You may decide to start paying more attention next time.

7. Expectations

Many people have found that they are more likely to dream, and more likely to remember those dreams, if they have made some initial preparations. Going to bed with a state of expectancy helps. Say to yourself, 'I will wake in the morning and remember my dreams.' Put a pen and paper by the bed, in readiness to record them.

Some people may ask for inspiration about something that is concerning them, and will go to sleep with a sense of expectancy that a dream will come in which some of the resources for dealing with the problem will be revealed.

While we are unable to make ourselves dream, we can at least prepare the ground, and be ready to do the work as the occasion arises.

8. Keeping Perspective

By making a conscious effort to record dreams, you will find that, with practice, dreams will occur in response to the amount of effort you put in. Some of the techniques outlined in chapter nine will also prove helpful.

Yet there will always be periods where you don't seem to recall your dreams. When these 'dry' patches occur, reflect on what has been happening in your everyday life. Have you been too busy to really pay attention? Have you unconsciously decided to 'switch off' for a while because some issues that have been arising require lots of energy or are a little too sensitive for you at present?

Be aware of your moods. Are you becoming irritable or short tempered, or feeling out of sorts? These may be signs that there are issues that are needing attention.

In this way, even the times where we seem not to dream can be opportunities for personal reflection and learning.

While keeping all these things in mind, however, it is important also to recognise that sometimes we may simply need the week off! Be gentle with yourself. Dreamwork has its best results when we are open to the experience and relaxed, yet have not turned it into another task to be accomplished. Resist the temptation to try to 'achieve'.

As with any other resource for personal or spiritual growth, a certain amount of self-discipline is required, yet the activity is not a goal or an end in itself. Our dreams are but one resource for the journey of living. Keeping a balance between the inner and outer life and a relaxed perspective are important elements in all such disciplines.

Notes

[1] Carroll, L. (Gardner, M. (ed.)) 1977. *The Annotated Alice*. Harmondsworth, Middlesex: Penguin. p.149.

RESOURCES FOR FURTHER REFLECTION

A. Glossary of Common Psychological Terms

Anima/animus The contrasexual side of the psyche. The animus is the masculine aspect of a woman's psyche; the anima is the feminine aspect of a man's psyche. Contrasexual figures also seem to be the source of religious and creative energy.

Archetype Themes, ideas and motifs representing basic human mental structures and/or abilities, perhaps related to universally experienced situations. According to Jung, they represent the fundamental inherited structures of our unconscious minds.

Collective unconscious The inherited material from all of human existence — symbols, abilities and archetypes that are held in common with the whole of humanity, throughout history and place. The collective unconscious exists independently of the individual's personal life experiences and affects how the latter are perceived.

Compensation The way that dreams (and other manifestations of the unconscious) are so often representations of those aspects of ourselves that we deny, or are unwilling to examine consciously.

Condensation A term devised by Freud to describe one's ability to put together, in a single dream, a whole collection of ideas and images from different times and areas of one's life. This is because all these ideas and images are bound together by a particular theme.

Depth psychology Theories and schools of psychology that emphasise unconscious processes and the investigation of people's most important inner attributes and problems.

Dream ego   The ego as experienced in dreams. This often seems to be the same as the waking ego, but sometimes perceives itself as less in control of events and less important than the waking ego.

Ego   The conscious identification and definition of oneself (the person that you think you are when you are awake!). The term originated with Freud, but is used by many non-psychoanalytic psychologists.

Ego consciousness   A similar term to ego, but emphasising the ego's role as conscious mediator of psychological functioning.

Introjection   Perceiving another's psychological material as though it were a part of oneself. It is the basis of much learning in childhood, but also a way of not perceiving negative attitudes towards oneself on the part of others. *You* then reject *them*, for example, instead of the other way round.

Persona   The 'public face' that we wear when in the presence of others — the mask(s) that we use every day. According to Jung, the assumption of a persona is a universal, unconscious, archetypal ability.

Projection   The opposite of introjection. Perceiving a forbidden thought or wish (or any part of the psyche that one is unaware of) in another person rather than oneself. For example, 'seeing' one's own contrasexual side in a member of the opposite sex.

Psyche   The mind or soul: a term much used by depth psychology.

Reaction formation   Preventing oneself from being aware of a forbidden thought or feeling by, instead, feeling precisely its opposite (the basis of most Mills & Boon romances).

Repression   Making something completely unavailable to consciousness so that, even when reminded of it, it means nothing to consciousness at all.

Secondary revision   The tendency for the conscious part of the mind to reorder or reconstruct a dream when retold, especially on a second or third retelling.

Self   In Jungian terminology, the central guiding archetype, giving purpose and direction to development, and at the core of the psyche (may be a model of, or pathway to, the external God).

Shadow   The archetypal 'alter ego' — the person we might have been but are not. The shadow contains many of our most important emotions and instincts, some at least of our potential for evil, and many repressed memories.

Subconscious   Anything 'below' the level of consciousness.

Unconscious   All of our psyche that our conscious mind is unaware of, including collective material. In depth psychology, it is generally regarded as the part of the mind that cannot easily be brought to consciousness by an act of will.

Unconscious defences   A concept of Freud's. The unconscious mind is said to use a variety of defensive techniques to prevent the conscious ego from being or becoming aware of forbidden desires or memories. The most important include: introjection, projection, reaction formation and repression.

B. Recommended Further Reading List

Biddulph, S. 1995. *Manhood*. Sydney: Tower Books.

Bly, R. 1990. *Iron John: A book about men*. Shaftesbury, Dorset: Element.

Brome, V. 1985. *Jung: Man and myth*. London: Paladin.

Brook, S. 1983. *The Oxford book of dreams*. Oxford: Oxford University Press.

Campbell, J. (ed.) *Myth, dreams and religion*. Dallas: Spring.

Clift, W. B. 1982. *Jung and Christianity: The challenge of reconciliation*. Melbourne: Collins Dove.

Clift, J. B. & Clift, W. B. 1989. *Symbols of transformation in dreams*. Melbourne: Collins Dove.

Edinger, E. 1986. *Encounter with the self*. Toronto: Inner City.

—— 1986. *The Bible and the psyche*. Toronto: Inner City.

—— 1987. *The Christian archetype*. Toronto: Inner City.

—— 1992. *Ego and archetype*. Boston: Shambala.

Fowler, J. W. 1981. *Stages of faith: The psychology of human development and the quest for meaning*. New York: HarperCollins.

Grant, W. H., Thompson, M. & Clarke, T. E. 1983. *From image to likeness: A Jungian path in the gospel journey*. Ramsey, NJ: Paulist Press.

Guggenbuhl-Craig, A. 1982. *Power in the helping professions*. Zurich: Spring.

—— 1995. *From the wrong side: A paradoxical approach to psychology*. Woodstock, CT: Spring.

Johnson, R. 1977. *He: Understanding masculine psychology*. New York: Harper & Row.

—— 1983. *We: Understanding the psychology of romantic love*. San Francisco: Harper & Row.

—— 1986. *Inner work: Using dreams and active imagination for personal growth*. San Francisco: Harper & Row.

—— 1987. *Ecstasy: Understanding the psychology of joy*. San Francisco: Harper & Row.

—— 1989. *She: Understanding feminine psychology*. New York: Harper & Row.

—— 1990. *Femininity lost and regained*. New York: HarperCollins.

—— 1991. *Owning your own shadow: Understanding the dark side of the psyche*. San Francisco: HarperCollins.

—— 1991. *Transformation: Understanding the dark side of the psyche*. San Francisco: HarperCollins.

—— 1993. *The fisher king and the handless maiden: Understand the wounded feeling function in masculine and feminine psychology*. San Francisco: HarperCollins.

Jung, C. G. 1957. *The undiscovered self*. New York: Penguin (Mentor).

—— 1958. *Modern man in search of a soul*. London: Routledge.

—— 1960. *On the nature of the psyche*. Princeton, NJ: Princeton University Press.

—— 1964. *Man and his symbols*. London: Aldus.

—— 1966. *The spirit in man, art and literature*. Princeton, NJ: Princeton University Press.

—— 1969. *Collected Works, 9i: The archetypes and the collective unconscious*. Princeton, NJ: Princeton University Press.

—— 1969. *Collected Works, 11: Psychology and religion: East and West*. Princeton, NJ: Princeton University Press.

—— 1974. *Dreams*. Princeton, NJ: Princeton University Press.

—— 1995. *Memories, dreams, reflections*. London: HarperCollins (Fontana).

Jung, E. 1957. *Animus and anima*. Dallas: Spring.

Keen, S. 1994. *Hymns to an unknown God: Awakening the spirit in everyday life*. New York: Bantam.

Koestler, A. 1964. *The act of creation*. London: Hutchinson.

Mattoon, M. 1978. *Understanding dreams*. Dallas: Spring.

Moore, T. 1992. *Care of the soul: A guide for cultivating depth and sacredness in everyday life*. New York: HarperCollins.

Neumann, E. 1972. *The great mother: An analysis of the archetype*. Princeton, NJ: Princeton University Press.

O'Connor, P. 1981. *Understanding the mid-life crisis*. Melbourne: Mandarin.

—— 1985. *Understanding Jung: Understanding yourself*. Melbourne: Mandarin.

—— 1992. *Dreams and the search for meaning*. Melbourne: Mandarin.

—— 1993. *The inner man: Men, myths, and dreams*. Sydney: Macmillan.

Peters, R. 1990. *Living with dreams*. London: Rider.

Pretat, J. R. 1994. *Coming to age: The croning years and late-life transformation*. Toronto: Inner City.

Price, S. & Thompson, D. 1993. *Think!: Working out what it means to be Christian*. Melbourne: JBCE.

Samuels, A. 1985. *The father: Contemporary Jungian perspectives*. New York: New York University Press.

Wilmer, H. A. 1994. *Understandable Jung: The personal side of Jungian psychology*. Wilmett, IL: Chiron.

C. Sample Rituals

The following rituals could be held in a church, in a small group setting or by an individual. Ideally, it is good to a have a special area set aside for such things — perhaps the corner of a spare room, with a low table and a candle left in place, though not all of us have the luxury of excess space for our own private 'chapel'! (These are Christian liturgies, but can be easily adapted for other religious perspectives.)

1. A liturgy for beginning dreamwork

Preparations: On the table or floor, place a candle or preferably an oil burner, and your journal, enclosed in some wrapping (or whatever you intend to record your dreams in), a poem/prose/quote (see below), and put on some inspirational music.

(Sit quietly, listening to your breathing, the music in the background, becoming aware of yourself and this space.)

Invitation: God of dreams and visions, I am here to begin a new venture. Wherever I journey, may your peace and love be my companions. *(The candle or oil burner is lit.)* May this light remind me that I will never be travelling alone. *(Silence.)*

Prayer: God, this is a new country for me, this land of dreams. I do not know its language, its customs, the roads to travel. Help me to find my way. Give me guides to travel with me, the encouragement of friends, and a supportive community. Help me to discover insight, wisdom and riches of the spirit as I go.

God, I'm not even sure what I will find. I am worried that I will not have enough dreams, and, if I do, they will be unfathomable, or that I may find I don't have the strength to listen to what my inner voice is saying. May I draw strength from you — the One who guided and inspired Joseph, Mary, Paul and all the other pilgrims of faith that have travelled this path before me.

May my dreaming, then, teach me of myself, that I may grow, and be a gift to others, too. Amen.

Dedication: *(Take the journal.)* This will be for me a special book. It is the place where I will place the gifts of my dreams. As it fills with words, pictures, ideas and feelings, may it take on a sacredness of its own, to be a special place where in Your company I undertake this deep spiritual journey. *(Undo the wrapping, and place the journal by the candle. You may wish to write your name, and perhaps a poem, quote or some prose that is special to you at this time.)*

I set aside this book for this task — a journal of my inner adventures. *(Silence.)*

Prayer for guidance: Journeying God, I ask for safety as I undertake my dreamwork. Help me not to become overwhelmed by my dreams, and to have the wisdom and humility to know when to ask for help, and when I am out of my depth … Guide me to the right people for advice and spiritual direction, and give me the courage to persevere when little seems to happen, when I get bored, or when there are things I don't want to face, yet need to learn. Keep me from getting so wrapped up in myself, and my inner journey, that I both forget my responsibilities to those around me, family and friends, and to take delight in the gifts of both company and solitude.

As I begin this venture, help me to have some beginning dreams that will point me in the way, and manner, in which I am to travel, and whether asleep or awake, may I rest assured of your love for me.

Blessing: The light of candles, the perfume of oil, fills this sacred space with a touch of your presence. May I now carry that peace into the rest of my day, at one with all Creation, and in expectation of the road ahead. Amen.

2. A liturgy for a disturbing dream

Preparation: Place a candle on a low table. You may want to have some quiet, contemplative music playing. In addition, you will need a small cloth, and a stone, roughly the size of your hand, and a small coin or gemstone.

(Sit quietly, listening to your breathing, the music in the background, becoming aware of yourself and this space.)

Beginning Prayer: Compassionate and Loving One, we come to this place seeking the comfort of your presence. As we light this candle, may the warmth and illumination of your company flood through each of us. *(The candle is lit, followed by a few moments of silence, as you listen to the music.)*

Prayer: God, you watch over us while we are asleep, and while we are awake. Today, peace eludes me, for the memories of my dreaming continue to live on into the daylight, confusing and confounding me. In this sacred space, I bring my dream to the Light, that you, as the God of Dreams, may help my understanding, and grant me inner peace.

The telling: Either to yourself, through writing, or by verbally retelling the dream to those present, the dream is brought into the open. *(If others are present, it is important to remember that this is not the place to offer interpretations, rather to encourage the dreamer to find the courage, peace and appropriate manner in which to work with the dream.)* You may wish to name specifically what elements of the dream disturb you.

Dedication: *(Take the stone and hold it in your hand, feeling its weight, texture and temperature. The following can be said by the dreamer or by another in the gathering.)*

This stone will be for me a symbol of my dream. Its weight reminds me of the manner in which this dream has unsettled me, and is weighing me down. Yet it may also be a gift of insight, learning and healing that awaits — I do not know. *(Take the cloth, and wrap the stone in it.)* To this end, I place the stone in safe-keeping, wrapping it carefully in this cloth, so that it may be respected, but is also enfolded in the protecting love of the Weaver God — the One who makes the tapestries of life. *(Place the stone on the table by the candle.)* Somewhere inside this stone may also be unknown treasure. So we place this coin (or gem) on top of the stone — to symbolise our hope and faith in the emerging wisdom and insight to be gained.

Prayer: God of Compassion, help us to work with our fears. May we trust in your peace and grace, asking that your love will banish our fear, giving us courage, insight and wisdom to continue on this unknown journey into this dream. Grant us peaceful and restful sleep this night, so that our strength will be restored, and that we will be enfolded in your love and care. And yet, may we also know, and not run away from, the right moment to begin to work with this experience, in order that we might continue to grow in faith, wisdom, compassion, love and wholeness.

Ending and blessing: Pass the peace to one another (clasping hands and saying: 'Peace be with you'; and responding, 'And also with you').

D. Biblical References: Dreams

But God came to Abimelech in a dream by night, and said to him, 'You are about to die because of the woman whom you have taken; for she is a married woman ...' — Gen. 20:ff

Then God said to him in the dream, 'Yes, I know that you did this in the integrity of your heart; furthermore it was I who kept you from sinning against me. Therefore I did not let you touch her.' — Gen. 20:6

And he dreamed that there was a ladder set up on the earth, the top of it reaching to heaven; and the angels of God were ascending and descending on it. — Gen. 28:12

During the mating of the flock I once had a dream in which I looked up and saw that the male goats that leaped upon the flock were striped, speckled and mottled. — Gen. 31:10

Then the angel of God said to me in the dream, 'Jacob,' and I said, 'Here I am!' — Gen. 31:11

But God came to Laban the Aramean in a dream by night, and said to him, 'Take heed that you say not a word to Jacob, either good or bad.' — Gen. 31:24

Once Joseph had a dream, and when he told it to his brothers, they hated him even more. — Gen. 37:ff

He had another dream, and told it to his brothers, saying, 'Look, I have had another dream: the sun, the moon, and eleven stars were bowing down to me.' — Gen. 37:9

'Come now, let us kill him and throw him into one of the pits; then we shall say that a wild animal has devoured him, and we shall see what will become of his dreams.' — Gen. 37:20

One night they both dreamed — the cupbearer and the baker of the king of Egypt, who were confined in the prison — each his own dream, and each dream with its own meaning. — Gen. 40:5

They said to him, 'We have had dreams, and there is no one to interpret them.' And Joseph said to them, 'Do not interpretations belong to God? Please tell them to me.' — Gen. 40:8

So the chief cupbearer told his dream to Joseph, and said to him, 'In my dream there was a vine before me …' — Gen. 40:9

When the chief baker saw that the interpretation was favourable, he said to Joseph, 'I also had a dream: there were three cake baskets on my head …' — Gen. 40:16

After two whole years, Pharaoh dreamed that he was standing by the Nile … — Gen. 41:1

Then he fell asleep and dreamed a second time; seven ears of grain, plump and good, were growing on one stalk. — Gen. 41:5

The thin ears swallowed up the seven plump and full ears. Pharaoh awoke, and it was a dream. — Gen. 41:7

In the morning his spirit was troubled; so he sent and called for all the magicians of Egypt and all its wise men. Pharaoh told them his dreams, but there was no one who could interpret them to Pharaoh. — Gen. 41:8

We dreamed on the same night, he and I, each having a dream with its own meaning. — Gen. 41:11

A young Hebrew was there with us, a servant of the captain of the guard. When we told him, he interpreted our dreams to us, giving an interpretation to each according to his dream. — Gen. 41:12

And Pharaoh said to Joseph, 'I have had a dream, and there is no one who can interpret it. I have heard it said of you that when you hear a dream you can interpret it.' — Gen. 41:15

Then Pharaoh said to Joseph, 'In my dream I was standing on the banks of the Nile …' — Gen. 41:17

I fell asleep a second time and I saw in my dream seven ears of grain, full and good, growing on one stalk ... — Gen. 41:22

Then Joseph said to Pharaoh, 'Pharaoh's dreams are one and the same; God has revealed to Pharaoh what he is about to do. — Gen. 41:25

The seven good cows are seven years, and the seven good ears are seven years; the dreams are one. — Gen. 41:26

And the doubling of Pharaoh's dream means that the thing is fixed by God, and God will shortly bring it about. — Gen. 41:32

Joseph also remembered the dreams that he had dreamed about them. He said to them, 'You are spies; you have come to see the nakedness of the land!' — Gen. 42:9

And he said, 'Hear my words: When there are prophets among you, I the LORD make myself known to them in visions; I speak to them in dreams. — Num. 12:6

If prophets or those who divine by dreams appear among you and promise you omens or portents ...' — Deu. 13:1

you must not heed the words of those prophets or those who divine by dreams; for the LORD your God is testing you, to know whether you indeed love the LORD your God with all your heart and soul. — Deu. 13:3

But those prophets or those who divine by dreams shall be put to death for having spoken treason against the LORD your God— who brought you out of the land of Egypt and redeemed you from the house of slavery — to turn you from the way in which the LORD your God commanded you to walk. So you shall purge the evil from your midst. — Deu. 13:5

When Gideon arrived, there was a man telling a dream to his comrade; and he said, 'I had a dream, and in it a cake of barley bread tumbled into the camp of Midian, and came to the tent, and struck it so that it fell; it turned upside down, and the tent collapsed.' — Judg. 7:13

When Gideon heard the telling of the dream and its interpretation, he worshiped; and he returned to the camp of Israel, and said, 'Get up; for the LORD has given the army of Midian into your hand.' — Judg. 7:15

When Saul inquired of the LORD, the LORD did not answer him, not by dreams, or by Urim, or by prophets. — 1 Sam. 28:6

Then Samuel said to Saul, 'Why have you disturbed me by bringing me up?' Saul answered, 'I am in great distress, for the Philistines are warring against me, and God has turned away from me and answers me no more, either by prophets or by dreams; so I have summoned you to tell me what I should do.' — 1 Sam. 28:15

At Gibeon the LORD appeared to Solomon in a dream by night; and God said, 'Ask what I should give you.' — 1 Ki. 3:5

Then Solomon awoke; it had been a dream. He came to Jerusalem where he stood before the ark of the covenant of the LORD. He offered up burnt offerings and offerings of well-being, and provided a feast for all his servants. — 1 Ki. 3:15

… then you scare me with dreams and terrify me with visions …' — Job 7:14

They will fly away like a dream, and not be found; they will be chased away like a vision of the night. — Job 20:8

In a dream, in a vision of the night, when deep sleep falls on mortals, while they slumber on their beds ...' — Job 33:15

They are like a dream when one awakes; on awaking you despise their phantoms. — Psa. 73:20

You sweep them away; they are like a dream, like grass that is renewed in the morning …' — Psa. 90:5

When the LORD restored the fortunes of Zion, we were like those who dream. — Psa. 126:1

For dreams come with many cares, and a fool's voice with many words. — Eccl. 5:3

With many dreams come vanities and a multitude of words; but fear God. — Eccl. 5:7

And the multitude of all the nations that fight against Ariel, all that fight against her and her stronghold, and who distress her, shall be like a dream, a vision of the night. — Isa. 29:7

Just as when a hungry person dreams of eating and wakes up still hungry, or a thirsty person dreams of drinking and wakes up faint, still thirsty, so shall the multitude of all the nations be that fight against Mount Zion — Isa. 29:8

Israel's sentinels are blind, they are all without knowledge; they are all silent dogs that cannot bark; dreaming, lying down, loving to slumber. — Isa. 56:10

I have heard what the prophets have said who prophesy lies in my name, saying, 'I have dreamed, I have dreamed!' — Jer. 23:25

They plan to make my people forget my name by their dreams that they tell one another, just as their ancestors forgot my name for Baal. — Jer. 23:27

Let the prophet who has a dream tell the dream, but let the one who has my word speak my word faithfully. What has straw in common with wheat? says the LORD. — Jer. 23:28

See, I am against those who prophesy lying dreams, says the LORD, and who tell them, and who lead my people astray by their lies and their recklessness, when I did not send them or appoint them; so they do not profit this people at all, says the LORD. — Jer. 23:32

You, therefore, must not listen to your prophets, your diviners, your dreamers, your soothsayers, or your sorcerers, who are saying to you, 'You shall not serve the king of Babylon.' — Jer. 27:9

For thus says the LORD of hosts, the God of Israel: Do not let the prophets and the diviners who are among you deceive you, and do not listen to the dreams that they dream ... — Jer. 29:8

To these four young men God gave knowledge and skill in every aspect of literature and wisdom; Daniel also had insight into all visions and dreams. — Dan. 1:17

In the second year of Nebuchadnezzar's reign, Nebuchadnezzar dreamed such dreams that his spirit was troubled and his sleep left him. — Dan 2:1

So the king commanded that the magicians, the enchanters, the sorcerers, and the Chaldeans be summoned to tell the king his dreams. When they came in and stood before the king ... — Dan. 2:2

He said to them, 'I have had such a dream that my spirit is troubled by the desire to understand it.' — Dan. 2:3

The Chaldeans said to the king (in Aramaic), 'O king, live forever! Tell your servants the dream, and we will reveal the interpretation.' — Dan. 2:4

The king answered the Chaldeans, 'This is a public decree: if you do not tell me both the dream and its interpretation, you shall be torn limb from limb, and your houses shall be laid in ruins. — Dan. 2:5

But if you do tell me the dream and its interpretation, you shall receive from me gifts and rewards and great honour. Therefore tell me the dream and its interpretation.' — Dan. 2:6

They answered a second time, 'Let the king first tell his servants the dream, then we can give its interpretation.' — Dan. 2:7

'If you do not tell me the dream, there is but one verdict for you. You have agreed to speak lying and misleading words to me until things take a turn. Therefore, tell me the dream, and I shall know that you can give me its interpretation.' — Dan. 2:9

The king said to Daniel, whose name was Belteshazzar, 'Are you able to tell me the dream that I have seen and its interpretation?' — Dan. 2:26

but there is a God in heaven who reveals mysteries, and he has disclosed to King Nebuchadnezzar what will happen at the end of days. Your dream and the visions of your head as you lay in bed were these … — Dan. 2:28

'This was the dream; now we will tell the king its interpretation.' — Dan. 2:36

just as you saw that a stone was cut from the mountain not by hands, and that it crushed the iron, the bronze, the clay, the silver, and the gold. The great God has informed the king what shall be hereafter. The dream is certain, and its interpretation trustworthy.' — Dan. 2:45

I saw a dream that frightened me; my fantasies in bed and the visions of my head terrified me. — Dan. 4:5

So I made a decree that all the wise men of Babylon should be brought before me, in order that they might tell me the interpretation of the dream. — Dan. 4:6

Then the magicians, the enchanters, the Chaldeans, and the diviners came in, and I told them the dream, but they could not tell me its interpretation. — Dan. 4:7

At last Daniel came in before me — he who was named Belteshazzar after the name of my god, and who is endowed with a spirit of the holy gods — and I told him the dream … — Dan. 4:8

'O Belteshazzar, chief of the magicians, I know that you are endowed with a spirit of the holy gods and that no mystery is too difficult for you. Hear the dream that I saw; tell me its interpretation. — Dan. 4:9

This is the dream that I, King Nebuchadnezzar, saw. Now you, Belteshazzar, declare the interpretation, since all the wise men of my kingdom are unable to tell me the interpretation. You are able, however, for you are endowed with a spirit of the holy gods.' — Dan. 4:18

Then Daniel, who was called Belteshazzar, was severely distressed for a while. His thoughts terrified him. The king said, 'Belteshazzar, do not let the dream or the interpretation terrify you.' Belteshazzar answered, 'My lord, may the dream be for those who hate you, and its interpretation for your enemies!' — Dan. 4:19

Because an excellent spirit, knowledge, and understanding to interpret dreams, explain riddles, and solve problems were found in this Daniel, whom the king named Belteshazzar. Now let Daniel be called, and he will give the interpretation.' — Dan. 5:12

In the first year of King Belshazzar of Babylon, Daniel had a dream and visions of his head as he lay in bed. Then he wrote down the dream ... — Dan. 7:1

Then afterward I will pour out my spirit on all flesh; your sons and your daughters shall prophesy, your old men shall dream dreams, and your young men shall see visions. — Joel 2:28

For the teraphim utter nonsense, and the diviners see lies; the dreamers tell false dreams, and give empty consolation. Therefore the people wander like sheep; they suffer for lack of a shepherd. — Zec. 10:2

But just when he had resolved to do this, an angel of the Lord appeared to him in a dream and said, 'Joseph, son of David, do not be afraid to take Mary as your wife, for the child conceived in her is from the Holy Spirit. — Mat. 1:20

And having been warned in a dream not to return to Herod, they left for their own country by another road. — Mat. 2:12

Now after they had left, an angel of the Lord appeared to Joseph in a dream and said, 'Get up, take the child and his mother, and flee to Egypt, and remain there until I tell you; for Herod is about to search for the child, to destroy him.' — Mat. 2:13

When Herod died, an angel of the Lord suddenly appeared in a dream to Joseph in Egypt and said ... — Mat. 2:19

But when he heard that Archelaus was ruling over Judea in place of his father Herod, he was afraid to go there. And after being warned in a dream, he went away to the district of Galilee. — Mat. 2:22

While he was sitting on the judgment seat, his wife sent word to him, 'Have nothing to do with that innocent man, for today I have suffered a great deal because of a dream about him.' — Mat. 27:19

'In the last days it will be, God declares, that I will pour out my Spirit upon all flesh, and your sons and your daughters shall prophesy, and your young men shall see visions, and your old men shall dream dreams. — Acts 2:17

Yet in the same way these dreamers also defile the flesh, reject authority, and slander the glorious ones. — Jude 1:8

E. Biblical References: Visions

After these things the word of the LORD came to Abram in a vision, 'Do not be afraid, Abram, I am your shield; your reward shall be very great.' — Gen. 15:1

God spoke to Israel in visions of the night, and said, 'Jacob, Jacob.' And he said, 'Here I am.' — Gen. 46:2

And he said, 'Hear my words: When there are prophets among you, I the LORD make myself known to them in visions; I speak to them in dreams. — Num. 12:6

The oracle of one who hears the words of God, who sees the vision of the Almighty, who falls down, but with eyes uncovered ... — Num. 24:4

The oracle of one who hears the words of God, and knows the knowledge of the Most High, who sees the vision of the Almighty, who falls down, but with his eyes uncovered ... — Num. 24:16

Now the boy Samuel was ministering to the LORD under Eli. The word of the LORD was rare in those days; visions were not widespread. — 1 Sam. 3:1

Samuel lay there until morning; then he opened the doors of the house of the LORD. Samuel was afraid to tell the vision to Eli. — 1 Sam. 3:15

In accordance with all these words and with all this vision, Nathan spoke to David. — 2 Sam. 7:17

In accordance with all these words and all this vision, Nathan spoke to David. — 1 Chr. 17:15

Now the rest of the acts of Solomon, from first to last, are they not written in the history of the prophet Nathan, and in the prophecy of Ahijah the Shilonite, and in the visions of the seer Iddo concerning Jeroboam son of Nebat? — 2 Chr. 9:29

Now the rest of the acts of Hezekiah, and his good deeds, are written in the vision of the prophet Isaiah son of Amoz in the Book of the Kings of Judah and Israel. — 2 Chr. 32:32

Amid thoughts from visions of the night, when deep sleep falls on mortals ... — Job 4:13

Then you scare me with dreams and terrify me with visions — Job 7:14

They will fly away like a dream, and not be found; they will be chased away like a vision of the night. — Job 20:8

In a dream, in a vision of the night, when deep sleep falls on mortals, while they slumber on their beds ... — Job 33:15

Then you spoke in a vision to your faithful one, and said: 'I have set the crown on one who is mighty, I have exalted one chosen from the people. — Psa. 89:19

The vision of Isaiah son of Amoz, which he saw concerning Judah and Jerusalem in the days of Uzziah, Jotham, Ahaz, and Hezekiah, kings of Judah. — Isa. 1:1

A stern vision is told to me; the betrayer betrays, and the destroyer destroys. Go up, O Elam, lay siege, O Media; all the sighing she has caused I bring to an end. — Isa. 21:2

The oracle concerning the valley of vision. What do you mean that you have gone up, all of you, to the housetops ... — Isa. 22:1

For the Lord GOD of hosts has a day of tumult and trampling and confusion in the valley of vision, a battering down of walls and a cry for help to the mountains. — Isa. 22:5

These also reel with wine and stagger with strong drink; the priest and the prophet reel with strong drink, they are confused with wine, they stagger with strong drink; they err in vision, they stumble in giving judgment. — Isa. 28:7

And the multitude of all the nations that fight against Ariel, all that fight against her and her stronghold, and who distress her, shall be like a dream, a vision of the night. — Isa. 29:7

The vision of all this has become for you like the words of a sealed document. If it is given to those who can read, with the command, 'Read this,' they say, 'We cannot, for it is sealed.' — Isa. 29:11

And the LORD said to me: The prophets are prophesying lies in my name; I did not send them, nor did I command them or speak to them. They are prophesying to you a lying vision, worthless divination, and the deceit of their own minds. — Jer. 14:14

Thus says the LORD of hosts: Do not listen to the words of the prophets who prophesy to you; they are deluding you. They speak visions of their own minds, not from the mouth of the LORD. — Jer. 23:16

A vision of all the women remaining in the house of the king of Judah being led out to the officials of the king of Babylon and saying, 'Your trusted friends have seduced you and have overcome you; Now that your feet are stuck in the mud, they desert you.' — Jer. 38:22

Her gates have sunk into the ground; he has ruined and broken her bars; her king and princes are among the nations; guidance is no more, and her prophets obtain no vision from the LORD. — Lam. 2:9

Your prophets have seen for you false and deceptive visions; they have not exposed your iniquity to restore your fortunes, but have seen oracles for you that are false and misleading. — Lam. 2:14

In the thirtieth year, in the fourth month, on the fifth day of the month, as I was among the exiles by the river Chebar, the heavens were opened, and I saw visions of God. — Ezek. 1:1

For the sellers shall not return to what has been sold as long as they remain alive. For the vision concerns all their multitude; it shall not be revoked. Because of their iniquity, they cannot maintain their lives. — Ezek. 7:13

Disaster comes upon disaster, rumour follows rumour; they shall keep seeking a vision from the prophet; instruction shall perish from the priest, and counsel from the elders. — Ezek. 7:26

It stretched out the form of a hand, and took me by a lock of my head; and the spirit lifted me up between earth and heaven, and brought me in visions of God to Jerusalem, to the entrance of the gateway of the inner court that faces north, to the seat of the image of jealousy, which provokes to jealousy. — Ezek. 8:3

And the glory of the God of Israel was there, like the vision that I had seen in the valley. — Ezek. 8:4

The spirit lifted me up and brought me in a vision by the spirit of God into Chaldea, to the exiles. Then the vision that I had seen left me. — Ezek. 11:24

Mortal, what is this proverb of yours about the land of Israel, which says, 'The days are prolonged, and every vision comes to nothing?' — Ezek. 12:22

Tell them therefore, 'Thus says the Lord GOD: I will put an end to this proverb, and they shall use it no more as a proverb in Israel.' But say to them, 'The days are near, and the fulfilment of every vision.' — Ezek. 12:23

For there shall no longer be any false vision or flattering divination within the house of Israel. — Ezek. 12:24

Mortal, the house of Israel is saying, 'The vision that he sees is for many years ahead; he prophesies for distant times.' — Ezek. 12:27

Have you not seen a false vision or uttered a lying divination, when you have said, 'Says the LORD,' even though I did not speak? — Ezek. 13:7

My hand will be against the prophets who see false visions and utter lying divinations; they shall not be in the council of my people, nor be enrolled in the register of the house of Israel, nor shall they enter the land of Israel; and you shall know that I am the Lord GOD. — Ezek. 13:9

The prophets of Israel who prophesied concerning Jerusalem and saw visions of peace for it, when there was no peace, says the Lord GOD. — Ezek. 13:16

Therefore you shall no longer see false visions or practice divination; I will save my people from your hand. Then you will know that I am the LORD. — Ezek. 13:23

Offering false visions for you, divining lies for you, they place you over the necks of the vile, wicked ones — those whose day has come, the time of final punishment. — Ezek. 21:29

Its prophets have smeared whitewash on their behalf, seeing false visions and divining lies for them, saying, 'Thus says the Lord GOD,' when the LORD has not spoken. — Ezek. 22:28

He brought me, in visions of God, to the land of Israel, and set me down upon a very high mountain, on which was a structure like a city to the south. — Ezek. 40:2

The vision I saw was like the vision that I had seen when he came to destroy the city, and like the vision that I had seen by the river Chebar; and I fell upon my face. — Ezek. 43:3

To these four young men God gave knowledge and skill in every aspect of literature and wisdom; Daniel also had insight into all visions and dreams. — Dan. 1:17

Then the mystery was revealed to Daniel in a vision of the night, and Daniel blessed the God of heaven. — Dan. 2:19

But there is a God in heaven who reveals mysteries, and he has disclosed to King Nebuchadnezzar what will happen at the end of days. Your dream and the visions of your head as you lay in bed were these … — Dan. 2:28

I continued looking, in the visions of my head as I lay in bed, and there was a holy watcher, coming down from heaven. — Dan. 4:13

In the first year of King Belshazzar of Babylon, Daniel had a dream and visions of his head as he lay in bed. Then he wrote down the dream … — Dan. 7:1

I, Daniel, saw in my vision by night the four winds of heaven stirring up the great sea … — Dan. 7:2

After this I saw in the visions by night a fourth beast, terrifying and dreadful and exceedingly strong. It had great iron teeth and was devouring, breaking in pieces, and stamping what was left with its feet. It was different from all the beasts that preceded it, and it had ten horns. — Dan. 7:7

As I watched in the night visions, I saw one like a human being coming with the clouds of heaven. And he came to the Ancient One and was presented before him. — Dan. 7:13

As for me, Daniel, my spirit was troubled within me, and the visions of my head terrified me. — Dan. 7:15

In the third year of the reign of King Belshazzar a vision appeared to me, Daniel, after the one that had appeared to me at first. — Dan. 8:1

In the vision I was looking and saw myself in Susa the capital, in the province of Elam, and I was by the river Ulai. — Dan. 8:2

Then I heard a holy one speaking, and another holy one said to the one that spoke, 'For how long is this vision concerning the regular burnt offering, the transgression that makes desolate, and the giving over of the sanctuary and host to be trampled?' — Dan. 8:13

When I, Daniel, had seen the vision, I tried to understand it. Then someone appeared standing before me, having the appearance of a man … — Dan. 8:15

And I heard a human voice by the Ulai, calling, 'Gabriel, help this man understand the vision.' — Dan. 8:16

So he came near where I stood; and when he came, I became frightened and fell prostrate. But he said to me, 'Understand, O mortal, that the vision is for the time of the end.' — Dan. 8:17

The vision of the evenings and the mornings that has been told is true. As for you, seal up the vision, for it refers to many days from now.' — Dan. 8:26

So I, Daniel, was overcome and lay sick for some days; then I arose and went about the king's business. But I was dismayed by the vision and did not understand it. — Dan. 8:27

While I was speaking in prayer, the man Gabriel, whom I had seen before in a vision, came to me in swift flight at the time of the evening sacrifice. — Dan. 9:21

At the beginning of your supplications a word went out, and I have come to declare it, for you are greatly beloved. So consider the word and understand the vision … — Dan. 9:23

'Seventy weeks are decreed for your people and your holy city: to finish the transgression, to put an end to sin, and to atone for iniquity, to bring in everlasting righteousness, to seal both vision and prophet, and to anoint a most holy place. — Dan. 9:24

In the third year of King Cyrus of Persia a word was revealed to Daniel, who was named Belteshazzar. The word was true, and it concerned a great conflict. He understood the word, having received understanding in the vision. — Dan. 10:1

I, Daniel, alone saw the vision; the people who were with me did not see the vision, though a great trembling fell upon them, and they fled and hid themselves. — Dan. 10:7

So I was left alone to see this great vision. My strength left me, and my complexion grew deathly pale, and I retained no strength. — Dan. 10:8

And have come to help you understand what is to happen to your people at the end of days. For there is a further vision for those days.' — Dan. 10:14

Then one in human form touched my lips, and I opened my mouth to speak, and said to the one who stood before me, 'My lord, because of the vision such pains have come upon me that I retain no strength. — Dan. 10:16

'In those times many shall rise against the king of the south. The lawless among your own people shall lift themselves up in order to fulfil the vision, but they shall fail. — Dan. 11:14

I spoke to the prophets; it was I who multiplied visions, and through the prophets I will bring destruction. — Hosea 12:10

The vision of Obadiah. Thus says the Lord GOD concerning Edom: We have heard a report from the LORD, and a messenger has been sent among the nations: 'Rise up! Let us rise against it for battle!' — Oba. 1:1

Therefore it shall be night to you, without vision, and darkness to you, without revelation. The sun shall go down upon the prophets, and the day shall be black over them ... — Micah 3:6

An oracle concerning Nineveh. The book of the vision of Nahum of Elkosh. — Nahum 1:1

Then the LORD answered me and said: Write the vision; make it plain on tablets, so that a runner may read it. — Hab. 2:2

For there is still a vision for the appointed time; it speaks of the end, and does not lie. If it seems to tarry, wait for it; it will surely come, it will not delay. — Hab. 2:3

On that day the prophets will be ashamed, every one, of their visions when they prophesy; they will not put on a hairy mantle in order to deceive ... — Zec. 13:4

As they were coming down the mountain, Jesus ordered them, 'Tell no one about the vision until after the Son of Man has been raised from the dead.' — Mat. 17:9

When he did come out, he could not speak to them, and they realised that he had seen a vision in the sanctuary. He kept motioning to them and remained unable to speak. — Luke 1:22

And when they did not find his body there, they came back and told us that they had indeed seen a vision of angels who said that he was alive. — Luke 24:23

Now there was a disciple in Damascus named Ananias. The Lord said to him in a vision, 'Ananias.' He answered, 'Here I am, Lord.' — Acts 9:10

And he has seen in a vision a man named Ananias come in and lay his hands on him so that he might regain his sight.' — Acts 9:12

One afternoon at about three o'clock he had a vision in which he clearly saw an angel of God coming in and saying to him, 'Cornelius.' — Acts 10:3

Now while Peter was greatly puzzled about what to make of the vision that he had seen, suddenly the men sent by Cornelius appeared. They were asking for Simon's house and were standing by the gate. — Acts 10:17

While Peter was still thinking about the vision, the Spirit said to him, 'Look, three men are searching for you.' — Acts 10:19

I was in the city of Joppa praying, and in a trance I saw a vision. There was something like a large sheet coming down from heaven, being lowered by its four corners; and it came close to me. — Acts 11:5

Peter went out and followed him; he did not realise that what was happening with the angel's help was real; he thought he was seeing a vision. — Acts 12:9

During the night Paul had a vision: there stood a man of Macedonia pleading with him and saying, 'Come over to Macedonia and help us.' — Acts 16:9

When he had seen the vision, we immediately tried to cross over to Macedonia, being convinced that God had called us to proclaim the good news to them. — Acts 16:10

One night the Lord said to Paul in a vision, 'Do not be afraid, but speak and do not be silent ...' — Acts 18:9

'After that, King Agrippa, I was not disobedient to the heavenly vision ...' — Acts 26:19

It is necessary to boast; nothing is to be gained by it, but I will go on to visions and revelations of the Lord. — 2 Cor. 12:1

Do not let anyone disqualify you, insisting on self-abasement and worship of angels, dwelling on visions, puffed up without cause by a human way of thinking ... — Col. 2:18

And this was how I saw the horses in my vision: the riders wore breastplates the colour of fire and of sapphire and of sulfur; the heads of the horses were like lions' heads, and fire and smoke and sulfur came out of their mouths. — Rev. 9:17

INDEX

Active Imagination *145–8*
Acts, Book of 32–3
Adler, Alfred 46
ancient traditions in dream analysis 3, 21–3, 76
anima/animus 60, *81-7*, 94–7, 113, 116, 123–5, *166*
Aquinas 36, 38, 53
archetypes, theory of *48*, 70–2, 86, 111–12, *166*
anima *81–7*, 94–7, 113, 116, *166*
  in dreams *81–7*, 94–7, 113, 116, *166*
animus *81–7*, 94–7, 113, 116, *166*
  in dreams *81–7*, 94–7, 113, 116, *166*
child *101–2*
  in dreams 102, 104, 127–9, 138
ego 44, 87, 112–14, 121–32, 137, 141, 144, *167*

in dreams 96, 131, 167
father *89–99*, 113
  in dreams 95
hero/heroine 76, 103, 113
  in dreams *103*, 130–2
mother *89–99*, 113
  in dreams 95
night journey *106*, 107
  in dreams 106, 107, 124, 129–32
persona *108*, 116, *167*
  in dreams 108
self *111–18*, *167*
  in dreams 108
shadow 75, 79, 108, *167*
  in dreams 75–9, 124–32
trickster *104–6*
  in dreams 104–6
wise old person *106–7*
  in dreams 106–7, 127–32
Aristotle 5, 65

art, dreams relationship with 8,
    53, 58, 76, 84
in dreamwork 148
Asceplius 5
Asia 5
associations
in dreams *42*, 122, 125, 135–9, 148
free association 42–3, 50, 136
Augustine 36
Augustus 5
Australia
dreams 39, 86, 107, 108, 125,
    129–131

'Beatty' Papyrus 4
Bible
dreams in Old Testament 8–21
dreams in New Testament 31– 4
texts 172–86

call dreams 54
child *see* archetypes, child
childhood
development 14, 75–76, 89–90,
    92–9, 113, 144
dreams 17
Christianity
faith 8, 9, 153–5
historical status of dreams 2, 31–9,
    45, 67–8
religious dreams 24–8, 31–4,
    106–7, 132
ritual 149(51
Cicero 6
collective unconscious 44–9, 76,
    107, 136–7, *166*
community

and dreams 4, 21, 56–7, 59–60, 115
and justice 22, 59–60
and responsibility 9, 26–7, 46,
    56–7, 59–60, 115, 153–5
compensation *26*, 34, *44*, 49, 78,
    105–6, *166*
condensation *43, 166*
context
biblical 23
in working with dreams 46–7, 138,
    154
conversion 115–17 (*see also*
    spirituality; God, in dreams)
creativity 8, 46, 57–8, 84, 85, 101,
    104, 114, 124

Daniel, Book of 28
death
in dreams 55, 96, 106
issues 103, 106–7, 112, 130–1, 139
demons, demonic 5, 36, 38, 77
depth psychology *166*
Deutoronomy, Book of 21–8
developmental stages 90, *111–18*
discernment and interpretation
    56, 116–17, 135–6
dragons 103
dreams
Biblical examples
    Old Testament 23–8
    New Testament 31–3
dreamwork/interpretation,
    difficulties and hazards of
    71–3, 139–41
emotional states 15, 16
history of 4–8, 21–39
people 57, 71, 84, 85, 95, 106–7,

121–32, 136–8, 144, 147, 149
psychological theories of *41–50*,
  66–70
religious theories of 9, 22–3, 27,
  33–7, 53–62
and stages of sleep 13–15
types of 53–7
Dream Interpretation Rules *see*
  rules

early church 34–7
Ecclesiasticus, Book of 33
Edinger, Edward 26, 73, 117
ego *see also* archetypes, ego *44*,
  75–6, 87, 90, 92, 111–14,
  121–32, 137, 141, 144, *166*, *167*
in dreams 96, 131, 167
ego-attitude 142–3, 167
self-axis 112
Electra complex *87*, 97
emotions in dreams 15, 16
erotic
content in dreams 3, 44, 82–4,
  94–9, 123–7, 144–5
ethics
in Active Imagination 146-7
and community 9, 26–7, 56–7
as expressed in dreams 56

fairy tales and stories, purpose
  of 7–8, 58, 67–9, 70–1, 79, 90,
  93, 103, 107, 113, 131, 137
faith 9, 115, 153–4 *see also*
  spirituality
fantasy 7–8, 68, 143, 163
father, *see* archetypes, father
Fowler, James 115

Freud, Sigmund *42–6*, 49, 97

God
and Christianity 8–10, 31–9,
  53–62, 153–5
in dreams 9, 23, 53–62, 90, 112,
  117
and religion 53–62
and self xiii, *112–18*
Greek, ancient culture and
  mythology 5
Gregory of Nyssa 36
group work *151–2*

Hebrew religion and dreams
  21–9, 34–5
hero/heroine, *see* archetypes,
  hero/heroine

illness and dreams 16
imagination 7, 8
see also creativity
active (*see* Active Imagination)
incarnation theology 59, 117
individuation
ego self-axis in 112
nature of *49–50*, 90, 117, 154
stages of 68, 108, 112–13, 117
introjection *167*
intuition 7, 47, 137
inversion 34

Jeremiah, Book of 27
Jerome 37–8
Jesus 32, 61, 154
Job, Book of 26, 117
Johnson, Robert 7, 81–2, 90, 142,

146–8
Joseph
in Book of Genesis 24–5
in Book of Matthew 31
journal, use of in dreamwork 135, 161–2
journey motif *106-7*, 124, 129–32, 149–50
Judaism (early) 34–5
Judges, Book of 25–6
Jung, Carl
and Freud 48–9
psychological theories *48–50*, 70–1, 75–6, 81–2, 102, 107, 111–13, 136, 145, 146–7
and religion ix, 1, 25
justice 22, 59–60

literal, literalism in dream interpretation 3, 16, 55–6, 82–3, 97
liturgy, in rituals 149–51, 170–2

Maeder 47
marriage 61, 94
in dreams 130–2
mask *see* persona
Matthew, Book of 31
mid-life crisis 112
monsters, in dreams 72, 95, 106
mother, *see* archetypes, mother

night terrors *17*
nightmares 17, 47, 93

Oedipus complex *87*, 97
omens 5

oracles 5

parental complexes 86–7, 92–3, 113, 125–6, 144
parenting 92–3, 144
persona *108*, 116, *167*
Plato 5
prayer 150–1, 170–2
projection *60*, 61, 82, 83, 85, 92, 94, 102, 113, 116, 123–4, 143, *167*
prophecy, in ancient traditions 5, 21–9, 37–8
prophetic dreams 22–8, 37, 54–6
psyche 49, 82, 108, 116, *167*
psychiatrists 5, 18, *156–7*
psychologists 5, 41–50, 59, *157*
psychology and spirituality xi, *58–62*, 114
psychotherapists 59, 157–8, *166*

rationalism 2, 6, 38–9
reality, and dream state 4, *15–17*, 82–3, 97
relationships 60, 61, 83, 87, 94, 98, 115, 143
religion/religious *see also* spiritual
outlook 8, 9, 53–62, 66–70, 115–18, 148–51, 153–5
religious dreams 22–3, 34, 54–6, 85
REM sleep *13–15*, 41–2
remembering dreams 13, 14, *161–5*
repression *167*
revelation 9, 22–3, 32, 56, 115–18
Revelation, Book of 33

ritual
creating 148–51
in dreams 131
examples 151, 170–2
purpose of *148–51*
Rivers, Dr W.H. 47
Roman, ancient culture and religion 5
rules
for dreamwork 72–3, 78, 82–3, 94, 98, 106–7, *135–44*
for recalling dreams *161–5*

secondary revision 44, *167*
self ix, 73, 108, *111–18*, *167*
and God image xiii, 112–18
sexuality
archetypes 77, 81–7, 98, 123–7
development 81
in dreams 44, 82–4, 94, 97, 99, 123–7, 144–5
shadow 60, *75–9*, 108, 124–132, *167*
sleep
REM sleep *13–15*, 41–2
sleep laboratories *13–15*, 41–2
stages of *13–15*, 41–2
Socrates 5
Solomon 24
spirituality xi-xiii, 2, 8–10, 15, 38, 46, 58–62, 69–70, 85, 113, 115–18, 148–51, 153–5, 162, 164
spiritual direction 108, 155–8
spiritual growth xi–xiii, 8–10, 46, 58–62, 76, 90, 106–8, 113, 115–18, 129–32, 148–51, 153–5
Stekel Wilhelm 47

superstition
ancient 5–6
modern 6, 38
symbolism xi, 5, 27, *43*, 57–8, 66, 150, 153
symbols, in dreams 3, 4, 7, 23, 44–5, 47, 48, 49, 92, 122, 127, 136–8, 143

Talmud 34–5
Tertullian 36
therapist
criteria *156–8*
in dreams 122
trickster, *see* archetypes, trickster
unconscious 34, *42–4*, 48–9, 76, 136–7, 139, 140, 143–9, *167 see also* collective unconscious

visions *28–9*, *32–3*
von Franz, Marie-Louise 55, 79

wholeness *115*, 155 *see also* individuation, spiritual growth
wise old person *see* archetypes, wise old person
worship, and ritual 149, 150, 170–2

Xenephones 5

* page numbers marked in italics indicate explanations of the main concepts or terms

0400771660 THI